The First 4 Years Are the Hardest

A Handbook for Campus Christians

Michael Pountney

InterVarsity Press
Downers Grove
Illinois 60515

© 1980 by Inter-Varsity Christian Fellowship of the United States of America

All rights reserved. No part of this book may be reproduced in any form without written permission from InterVarsity Press, Downers Grove, Illinois.

InterVarsity Press is the book-publishing division of Inter-Varsity Christian Fellowship, a student movement active on campus at hundreds of universities, colleges and schools of nursing. For information about local and regional activities, write IVCF, 233 Langdon St., Madison, WI 53703.

Distributed in Canada through InterVarsity Press, 1875 Leslie St., Unit 10, Don Mills, Ontario M3B 2M5, Canada.

HOLY BIBLE New International Version, Copyright © 1978, New York International Bible Society, Used by permission.

Cover illustration by Kurt Mitchell; interior illustrations by Dave Zentner

ISBN 0-87784-451-8

Printed in the United States of America

Library of Congress Cataloging in Publication Data

Pountney, Michael.
    The first four years are the hardest.

    Includes bibliographies.
    1.   College students—Conduct of life.   I.   Title.
LB3605.P577   378'.198   80-19792
ISBN 0-87784-451-8

18	17	16	15	14	13	12	11	10	9	8	7	6	5	4	3	2
95	94	93	92	91	90	89	88	87	86	85	84	83	82	81		

With gratitude, this book is dedicated to the IVCF students at the University of Victoria, British Columbia, to whom I was apprenticed; and to my daughters, Michelle and Christine, who so ingenuously encouraged their daddy to try and become a "famous author"; and to my wife, Elaine, who did not type a word of the manuscript but loves me beyond words.

I Know Exactly Where You Are

I know exactly where you are right now. Well, some of you. You're sitting with your back against the wall in a far corner of the college cafeteria.

The place is called the Sub, the Pit, the Barn or some such name. It is surprisingly dirty. In the middle of the table, beneath the rubble of butts and beers, there is a folded, printed notice wearily pleading with you to stack your own dishes. But no one has since the place opened at eight-thirty this morning.

Behind you, stapled, tacked, gummed or pinned, are hundreds of notices and advertisements. Leftover summer-session exam schedules, offers of used textbooks and hundred-dollar cars with the seller's phone number on little vertical strips at the bottom. Wise vendors tear off a few strips themselves to make the ad look as if other students are sensible enough to have already taken interest.

Around you, people are talking animatedly, reading silently or sleeping peacefully, their heads on their arms and their hair brushing the spilled dark coffee from overturned styrofoam cups. This man on your left is obviously a professor; the leather elbow patches are planted firmly on the table, and he puffs placidly on his pipe while he reads a slim, well-worn volume. You strain to read the title, *Metaphysical Poetry.*

The woman over there is different. She looks startlingly young. Sandals hang from the toes of her outstretched feet and her caftan trails lazily in the dust of the tiled floor. You don't know it, but she's a professor too.

It's two-thirty in the afternoon, and you've just completed registering for your year at school. At last.

Remember how it all began? You had been thinking of college for a long time, discussing the possibilities with your parents, checking opinions from your older brother, asking your friends if they thought it would be OK and praying a lot for guidance.

Then in response to your innocent request for information about admission, you received that exciting brown package. A hundred-page catalog promised you courses in anything from anthropology to zoology, although you needed to write back with a special request if you wanted the supplementary booklet on the Graduate Department of Afghan Poetry.

The registrar demanded the usual transcripts, and you anxiously remembered your bad marks in French 11 and Math 12. You wondered if this paperwork was all necessary.

Also included was information about health services and the VD clinic and advice on buying textbooks. There were pages of information about bursaries and scholarships and student loans, with a late addendum noting that Local 416 of the Teamsters' Union had created a Minority Award in Transportation Studies, available to any Jewish mother of two, the only prerequisites being a professional chauffeur's license and a postsecondary diploma in heavy-duty mechanics.

Today you have finally completed your registration. You've lined up in a dozen lines in a dozen different buildings from one end of campus to the other. You've found that Biology 214 (Cell Biology: Structural Basis) is full, and you've had to settle for Biology 216 (Microscopy and Histology), and you don't even know what histology is. You've found that the pre-req for Spanish 212 is Spanish 213 and that the pre-req for Spanish 213 is Spanish 212. And nobody cares.

You've got your plasticized library card with your photo and student I.D. number. The photo is awful but nobody cares about that either. You've paid your activities fee and found out when the racquetball courts are free. You've bought one huge physics textbook that cost over twenty dollars (not knowing that this year's professor thinks it's outdated and will never use it) and a great wad of yellow refill paper for your binder.

You have become a student, and you are ready to start college for the first time in your life. But nobody seems to have noticed much.

If you are one of the lucky ones, there has been at least one encouraging sign for you today, an indication that you, as a Christian, are not going to be totally alone on this campus. As you lined up in the administration building to pay your fees, a guy thrust a flyer into your hand and rattled off something about the Christian fellowship welcoming you to campus.

As you shuffled anonymously forward in the line toward the "Pay Fees Here—Cash Only" notice, you cautiously read the announcement. The Christian group was running an orientation evening for new students, eh? Next Friday in the Gold Room in the Union. Free supper too. You wanted to go and talk to the guy who gave you the notice, but that meant leaving your place in line and showing him that you were interested: the former would be foolish, the latter unsafe. Besides, he had stopped giving the leaflets out and was laughing and talking with a good-looking gal about thirty places behind you. So you rewrapped yourself in the comforting cloak of anonymity and shuffled forward another step.

A Career Christian?

Now, sitting in the cafeteria, a real student in a real college, you're slightly apprehensive. Not so much about your college career (although you *would* like to be a Rhodes Scholar) as about your Christian career. What is it going to be like, being a follower of Jesus on this very secular campus?

You remember some of the rumors and stories you've heard about the anti-Christian stance of teachers and students, about young Christians being mocked and scorned when they've stood up for creationism, about young people from your church who just tossed their faith aside and dived headlong into the student world of pleasure and apathy, of timid followers losing courage, and faithful high-schoolers becoming faithless.

What do you need to know to help you remain firm and steadfast in your Christian life? What sort of advice and encouragement do you need? Is there any help at all?

This book was written to do just that: to encourage and advise Christian students as they begin and continue their university careers. This book is designed as a sort of handbook, the kind of book a soldier takes into battle or a mechanic uses to troubleshoot a problem engine. It will strengthen your courage and resolve; it will encourage you and enthuse you, and it will give you some of the equipment you need to solve the problems of living a strong Christian witness on campus.

This book, however, is neither the complete answer to all your problems nor the only one. It can never substitute for the flesh-and-blood friends who will walk with you in your Christian stride or for the wholly real energy that comes from the Spirit of God, who, having begun the good work in you, "will carry it on to completion until the day of Christ Jesus" (Phil. 1:6).

How This Book Will Help

Your college career is going to start early next Monday morning, with an eight-thirty class in math. And for a few days you will simply be overwhelmed with the multifold details of getting to the right building for the right class on the right day at the right time. But as your head begins to surface from the morass of new facts toward the end of the first week, shake it clear and think about getting the really important things organized.

This book suggests that the basic props of any Christian life are fellowship and the Daily Quiet Time. Find where the other Christians are and join them. Go to that Christian orientation meeting you saw advertised. You really need to meet those Christians: I doubt if you will survive by yourself. Those other believers are vital to your health; the free supper is merely incidental.

A firmly established Quiet Time along with Christian fellowship won't guarantee that your year will be without problems and new challenges. But they will give you a base on which to meet those challenges. You might run into one of those particularly hostile professors—the ones who decided to teach college because they hate kids. There's help in this book too for dealing with them. And by December, you may find that your schedule is so full of appointments, dates, events and commitments that you're tempted to apply for hermit school and become a recluse. Don't despair! Read chapter five.

Chapter six may be the one you'll need around the end of January. That's often the time when students begin to feel comfortable with the routine and have some time to take a breather. As you lift your nose from the grindstone you may get a whiff of temptation. And depending on the strength of those temptations, you may begin to worry about your sanity. Are you normal? Do other people struggle with the same thoughts that embarrass and oppress you so much? Chapter seven may be of some help as you grapple with the feeling of being weird.

As your heart warms to thoughts of summer, you might be looking for some guidelines for planning your vacation. How can you make the best of those three long months of play . . . and work? And while you're contemplating the end of the year, you might be reflecting on how you've done. Was it a good year? a growing year? a maturing year? Did you succeed as a Christian student? That all depends on what you mean by success. The final chapter of this book deals with that. You'll have a standard for evaluation that comes from the New Testament and not from the warped measuring rods of this age.

The year ahead will not be as long as it now may seem. In eight months you'll be packing your tennis racket and dropping off term papers as you head into the May sunshine. And after that you'll only have three more years to get through. Then you're home free, because the first four years are the hardest. And if this book has helped you in any way during these years to grow in obedience, faithfulness and courage, then the prayers of the author will have been more than answered.

He'll Be Reading
a Copy of *The Times*
Upside Down

I've always loved those spy stories in which there is a mysterious, surreptitious rendezvous between the spy and his contact. In John Le Carré's book *The Honourable Schoolboy,* [1] when the British spy Jerry Westerby is reactivated for an assignment in East Asia, a clandestine rendezvous is arranged for him in London with the head of British security, George Smiley. Jerry is to wait at a particular bus stop in Green Park, carrying a paper shopping bag from Fortnum and Mason. By some elusive process he is to always remain at the back of the line. Eventually a battered Bedford van appears, carrying a ladder on its ancient green roof and the legend "Harris—Builders" on its sides.

"Where's Wilf, then?" the driver gruffly demands.

"You'll have to make do with me," says Westerby, and climbs in.

The contact is made and the serious games begin.

Often in such secret meetings the contact is recognizable by some external mark: he is wearing a very old black beret or sporting a white carnation in his right buttonhole or reading a copy of *The Times* upside down. Such things have always excited

me and led me into fanciful imaginings of sauntering noncha-
lantly down the Kurfürstendamm, picking my teeth with the
sawn-off half of an opera ticket and awaiting Natasha, the leather-
clad romantic legend of the NKVD.

In some respects, when a brand-new Christian student slides
furtively into English 101 he or she is like a spy operating deep
inside enemy territory. Around are dozens, hundreds of foreign
counterintelligence agents, men and women in the pay of the

enemy. These people are easy to recognize: their speech, their behavior, sometimes even their looks betray them. Soon will enter the archenemy himself—that professor of counterintelligence—the literature teacher. How, cries the student in agony, can I recognize those people who are on my side? Where are the other Christians?

Identifying Christians in Enemy Territory

The campus is like enemy territory. It is a pagan educational complex serving the needs and exhibiting the styles of a godless culture. As such, Satan, that old enemy, reigns unheeded and unhindered. And you, a follower of Jesus in the service of a greater and higher Intelligence, are a lone agent penetrating the fortress of the enemy. You need not stay alone, though. Psssst. Come closer. "There are more of us in Physics 120."

How do you identify other believers? Well, there are no external signs in the obvious sense: no second-birth marks, no plastic halos hovering magically above the hair, no fledgling wings on the shoulder blades. There is nothing like what happens to Dorothy in *The Wizard of Oz*. After she has accidentally—and apologetically—killed the wicked witch of the east by having the house fall on her, she meets the good witch of the north. We know she's the good witch because she's got a silver crown and carries a silver wand and all the children cheer when she comes in (at least that's what happened in the special version I saw in Victoria last Christmas). Maybe that's what Christians could do: wear silver crowns and carry wands. At least people who go to plays would know we were on the good side.

The good witch gives Dorothy a mark to wear on her forehead to show that she is under magic protection. A blue triangle is stuck on Dorothy's forehead, right between the eyes, much to the delight and amazement of the Munchkins who happen to be watching all this. Great. Now everyone knows whose side Dorothy is on.

Are there any clues like this in looking for Christians in your classes? A mournful step, perhaps? A big, black Bible in a plain brown wrapper? Calluses on the knees? Scars from too much fighting the good fight? Unfortunately for secret agent F.R.O.S.H. there are no indicators of this overt kind.

Special Identification Marks

However, there are some signs by which you can identify people and know their loyalties.[2] Just as you recognize the enemy by his speech and behavior, so you recognize fellow believers by the same things. But there's got to be more than that. What is really different about the way Christians act?

There is one special feature that sets off the speech and behavior of a Christian. Remembering that enemy counteragents are good at subterfuge and deception, we will not allow ourselves to be misled by phoney words or the pretense of action. We are looking for that one, authentic, infallible method of detecting who is on our side, and this is it: Does the man or woman live a lifestyle of love?

Francis Schaeffer wrote a gem of a book called *The Mark of the Christian*. His theme boils down to one very simple point: you recognize Christians by the fact that they love with a fierce, extraordinary love.

Jesus himself said that this would be the sign. "All men will know that you are my disciples if you love one another" (Jn. 13:35). That is the trademark of the followers of Jesus, as distinctive as the three stripes on a pair of Adidas running shoes, as visible as the huge, golden arches at a McDonald's.

The love that Jesus speaks of is never offered to us as an option, as an item that we can tack onto the standard chassis of discipleship if we wish. Continually, in page after page of Scripture, we are commanded to love. It's the very top line in all our sealed orders. "This is my command," says Jesus. "Love each other" (Jn. 15:17).

So as you take notes in your first few sociology lectures, keep a secret watch to see if there's anyone who bears the mark of love.

How does it show? In little ways to begin with. In a smile and that calm sense of security that a certain student shows. In the offer to pick up that text for you at the bookstore. In the generous favor of a ride home, a place to sleep, a meal to share. In the most concrete and practical ways, the Christian mark of love irresistibly works its way out of the corner into the center of the ring.

As the sociology course develops, the trademark grows easier to read. It's love that picks up on the quiet kid at the back who seems so lost and bewildered by everything. It's love that finds out that the reason Jane is so pale and sad is that her mother is dying, and love brings comfort. It's love that encourages the weaker students and shares time and understanding with them.

That's what you're looking for. Find those people, the ones who are on your side and join up with them. Develop a pocket of resistance and become a guerrilla army. Fortified by numbers, even the most disheartened secret agents can begin to encourage and strengthen each other and fight back.

I'll always remember a ginger-haired guy called Keith. He was in my classes during my first year at a Teacher Training College in London. He was a tremendously attractive person because he was so interested in life and so downright good. I was a timid secret agent, looking desperately for Christian allies, and I found Keith.

His kindness and friendliness first identified him. He endorsed goodness wherever he found it but quizzically questioned things that were wrong. He was an enthusiastic treasurer of the Wrestling Club but bravely spoke out when the national champion stole some equipment. He was courageous, enthusiastic and he cared for people.

We became fast friends, bound by our shared faith in Jesus. His dorm became my second home. We plotted prayerful strategy against some of the rottenness around us. He mended guys' cars and even ironed their shirts. He was Christ's man and it showed.

I am privileged to have met many of the secret agents on

campus at the University of Victoria. Last spring, just prior to finals, two women students were burned out of their apartment and lost all their texts and notes. The Inter-Varsity students heard about this on the news. Within twenty-four hours they had rounded up duplicate texts and people willing to share their notebooks. That's love.

Finding and Being Found

Secret signs and passwords serve a dual purpose. They allow you to find your contact, and they allow your contact to find you. Spy stories have the following classic way of arranging the clandestine rendezvous of two agents who are unknown to each other. Each party is given half of a torn dollar bill or ticket and the task is to match up the two halves when the right people meet. This principle is good for matching you up with the other believers on campus.

As you walk around the university with the mark of love clenched in your fist like the torn half of a secret ticket, you'll meet people who have the matching half. There will be students and professors whose mark of love is the same as yours. Now there are two ways to get the matching halves together.

The first way is the way of caution. This is like sitting in the crowd at a soccer game. Although one team has only ten players and it seems as if they're wearing the same colors as you, you timidly watch from the sidelines for eighty-nine minutes. Then, when you're absolutely sure that this is the team you're supposed to be on, you race out and join them for the final minute. After all, it's safe enough by now—they're winning by three goals.

The second way is for the brave. This is the better way: "For God did not give us a spirit of timidity, but a spirit of power, of love and of self-discipline" (2 Tim. 1:7). Undismayed by the size of your opponents, undaunted by the probability of getting wiped out by the league leaders, you race onto the field. "Who's on my side?" you cry as you kick off. And from the dressing-room tunnel sprint out ten classmates to join you on the field.

Whatever happens, whether you play three short or have a dozen reserves, you must get into the game at once. You are under orders to hold up the matching half of the mark of love.

Poor Clark Kent could never reveal his true identity as Superman, not even to Lois Lane. No one ever knew that the mild-mannered reporter was leading a double life. Many of us followers of Jesus like to stay hidden as mild-mannered pagans, unwilling—not unable, but unwilling—to show ourselves in our true colors as Christians. The Bible knows nothing of such secret agents who are too fearful to let their love show or meet up with other agents.

What to Do when You Find Another Agent
Secret agents are sent into enemy territory for a variety of reasons: to destroy installations, to retrieve information or to rescue people from enemy hands.

Your purpose as a Christian agent is to rescue people from enemy darkness and bring them over to the kingdom of light. It's hard to do this sort of work alone. It's easier and more effective if you link up with other agents.

You'll find them easily enough, though some of them are unlikely people in unlikely places. In our local enemy territory, the U. of Victoria, we've got secret agents in the symphony orchestra (six of them!) and on the library staff, in the counseling department and doing physics research, directing the clubs council and staffing the records office. When you find them, work with them on the rescue mission.

The Risks of Secret Service
Any secret agent who is courageous enough to infiltrate enemy lines and hang up his secret sign (no matter how supposedly secret that sign may be) is taking a horrendous risk. The risk is that his secret sign may be known to the enemy and that he will be caught.

William Stevenson's history of the secret war of 1939-45, the book *Intrepid,* is filled with such cases. One of the saddest concerns a beautiful English spy whose code name was Madeleine. She was parachuted into France to set up a secret radio link between the resistance fighters in Paris and her home base in London. But even as she landed, the Gestapo knew that an Allied reinforcement had arrived.

The Gestapo hunted her, intercepting her coded phone calls and beaming in on her secret radio messages until the net closed around a certain Paris apartment. There she was arrested.

So there are great disadvantages in this Wizard of Oz, blue-triangle thing. Although it's a great way to identify you to your friends, it's also a great way to betray you to your enemies. And remember where Dorothy's sign was—right between the eyes. Perfect for getting shot at. So that's the risk. If you hang up your less-than-secret sign of love and defend it with a clear articulation of what you believe, you make yourself a great target for getting shot at. Or being mocked and ridiculed.

It would be much safer to hide, to take off the blue triangle and conceal it in your biology text, not to let your fierce love for people show. But you can't. You're already hooked on this heady stuff of discipleship. You and I have no choice now; we have to hang out our signs.

This compulsion to be visible, this inner drive to show our faith comes out strongly in the lives of such biblical people as Jeremiah, Peter and Paul. In Jeremiah 20, the prophet cries that there is no way he can hold back his prophecies. "But if I say, 'I will not mention him or speak any more in his name,' his word is in my heart like a burning fire, shut up in my bones. I am weary of holding it in; indeed, I cannot" (v. 9).

In Acts 5, the moment Peter and his friends have been rescued from prison, having been forbidden to preach publicly, they're back out on the streets doing the very same thing. They can't resist it. "We must obey God rather than men!" exclaims Peter (v. 29). To Paul, the irresistibility is so logical. "I believed;

therefore I have spoken." "I am compelled to preach" (2 Cor. 4:13; 1 Cor. 9:16).

It cost these men something—beatings and jailings. Letting your sign of love show in front of your class will probably cost you something. As you try to find your fellow agents, you might get hurt. But the command to show love and the need to find the others who are on your side are imperatives. The orders are inescapable. You can't be God's agent without love.

So when you've got half a hunch that the girl in the fourth row in sociology is a secret agent like you, creep up behind her one day and whisper in your best spy's accent, "Are you one of us?" If she answers yes, rejoice and welcome your fellow conspirator.

Suggested reading:
White, John. "On Being a Signpost," chapter 4 of *The Fight.* Downers Grove, Ill.: InterVarsity Press, 1976.
Milne, Bruce. *We Belong Together: The Meaning of Fellowship.* Downers Grove, Ill.: InterVarsity Press, 1978.
Benjamin, Barbara. *The Impossible Community: A Story of Hardship and Hope at Brooklyn College in New York.* Downers Grove, Ill.: InterVarsity Press, 1978.

3

DQT Your Regular Dose of DQT

Lest you choke on your Dairy Queen hamburger or waste fifteen minutes reading this chapter to find out what the title means, let me explain it right away. DQT stands for two things: Don't Quit Taking and Daily Quiet Time. Therefore, as you linguists and interpreters have already concluded, this chapter title in longhand means, "Don't Quit Taking Your Regular Dose of Daily Quiet Time."

So while you are still groaning over that awful, cutesy play on initials, I'll try to answer your first question: Why?

The Lifeline Link

Good question. Why do followers of Jesus need to set aside time each day to pray and study the Bible, to be alone with God and listen to him speak? In some respects the answers are too simple to bother mentioning. You need a DQT because it is literally your lifeline with the living God. It is direct communication between you and him. He can hear your voice; you can hear his. "The voice of the LORD is powerful; the voice of the LORD is majestic" (Ps. 29:4).

The DQT is the most direct way for you to come into your Father's presence. Practiced and developed over the years, it becomes a disciplined habit that builds strong Christian muscles. It lets the Father know that you are serious in your intention to be with him, to listen to him and have him guide you. It gives God a daily opportunity to contact you and pass on any messages he may have.

It's similar to the daily radio contacts racing sponsors make with yachtsmen who are sailing single-handedly across the Atlantic in such races as the French "Route de Rhum."

Starting at St. Malo on the Brittany coast of northern France, the solo skippers race the four thousand miles of green Atlantic to Guadeloupe in the French Caribbean. Amazingly, in the 1979 race, the smallest entry, an eleven-meter trimaran beat the largest competitor, a twenty-one-meter monohull, by only one minute thirty-five seconds. All the time the fleet was at sea, they were watched over by a communications ship and planes from the French navy.

That is how the organizers of the race insure daily contact with the boats as each skipper tracks his lonely, great circle route to the Caribbean.

Can you imagine how important those daily radio broadcasts are to the isolated sailors? They provide weather reports and details of the other challengers; they bring the voices of family members into the cockpit of the boat; they bring news of the rest of the world, medical advice, warnings and encouragement; they bring music and entertainment. The radio hookups are equally important to the people back at home base. The families long for a chance to chat with their loved ones; the organizers are anxious to keep a safety check on each boat; supervisors need to remain in control of the total situation.

This is an image of what Daily Quiet Time means to both us and God. And because the DQT spans two worlds, it is more vital than any communication link between parties of a single world.

DQT Proves WMB

The DQT is also proof: proof that we are serious in what we say we are committed to. Thus as we tenaciously and resolutely practice our DQT, sometimes through clenched teeth, sometimes at an unearthly hour of the morning, sometimes with knees that are stiff from floor hockey, sometimes with the tears of tragedy and ugly memories, sometimes with high boredom or a dryness that would make the gardens at Versailles Palace seem like the Kalahari Desert, we prove to the Father that we are determined to get to know him and to live constantly with him. In other words, the DQT also stands for WMB—We Mean Business.

And such proof, offered daily and consistently, does not go unrewarded. God, in his turn, puts his stamp of approval on our lives. And by his work, what starts off like the thin, invisible filament of a radio link is woven into the strands of an underwater cable. The slim thread becomes a thick wire rope.

It's Yours; Take It with You

As well as simple communication, as well as proof that you're serious about knowing God, the DQT is also the best way to build into your life the individuality that your faith needs to be strong and to stand the test of ridicule. You may ride on the coattails of a young people's group or an I-V chapter or any intimate Christian community you can name, but as it is alone that you are born and die, so it is alone that your faith must be measured and tested. Stripped of all the societal supports and the bottle feeding of your Christian friends, what is left to sustain you? Answer . . . the DQT.

The Daily Quiet Time is immensely portable; you can take it anywhere with you, even on airplanes. It fits easily under the seat. It's quiet and unobtrusive, well behaved and appropriate in all circumstances. It's available at all times of the day, open for business like any twenty-four-hour laundry. It's cheap and demands little servicing. It is thoroughly and absolutely yours.

"Sorry, ma'm, your DQT will have to ride in the baggage compartment."

As in a foot race, when you strip off your track suit and leave behind your fancy training schedules and your bioenergized breakfast cereals, there is only you left, to make it or break it. So also when you strip off your Christian meetings and your small group prayer partners there is left only you and your DQT. It is the measure of a Christian man or woman.

"How am I doing in the faith?" you ask.

"Tell me about your personal Daily Quiet Time," I answer.

How Does a DQT Work?
You have to work to make your Quiet Time come alive and stay alive. Most beginners have trouble with this, so don't despair if you do too. As you get a few miles farther down the road the whole thing becomes easier. I'm not sure exactly why. I think it

must be because you get to know the person at the other end so much better. The aim is to make the DQT so lively and scintillating that it is difficult to stop yourself from getting down on your knees all over the place and equally hard to heave yourself off them and get back into the real world.

What an astonishingly bad phrase that last one is. Contact with the living, soul-searing God *is* the real world. All else—the concrete campus and the crowded cafeterias, the basketball and the books—all else is shadow.

How do you make your DQT a lively affair? What do you actually do? There are no traditional methods written in letters of stone; there is no liturgy inscribed on the dormitory wall, no grooves on the floor facing east into which you have to fit your knees. All this vague waffle about talking to God and listening to him leaves you cold. What do you actually do?

Time
One of the best things you can do is structure your Quiet Times. Whip them into shape; cut out a pattern; draw up a list of contents. Then you'll know what your DQT is. The first structure I would suggest is that of time.

Six o'clock in the morning is not a hallowed hour, blessed specially by God and set apart for the particularly righteous (with extra blessing if you start at 5:30). There is no great intrinsic value in having a morning Quiet Time as opposed to an evening one. Value lies in regularity. Underline the *D* in DQT. Choose a suitable time of the day or night and sign up for a tutorial with God. Make it easy on yourself; it doesn't have to hurt to be effective. As a teen-ager I thought that if I prayed at 5:00 in the morning God would be so impressed with me that my brownie-point score in heaven would take quantum leaps forward. All that happened was that I fell asleep after my opening "Dear Lord" and felt spiritually wretched and physically shattered for the rest of the day. So choose a comfortable time of day.

A miserable, year-long enslavement to seventeen minutes between the pillow and the toothpaste is not necessarily the best method. Change things as you go along. Experiment. Use the late morning, early evening, the time between classes, the bus to campus. A friend used to read his pocket New Testament as he cycled to campus. He thought, though, that his method detracted from his prayer life as all he could manage was a few arrow prayers that he wouldn't get hit by a truck. Mornings are certainly excellent. But if you're a night owl, perhaps a rendezvous between midnight and one is the best approach.

Now I've frightened you because I've suggested that the DQT should take an hour. Well, should it?

Of course not. The very essence of free communication with the Lord we love is that it is beyond slavish format. You don't need to make a contract and punch in and out like an assembly-line worker. If you are new to the idea, practice with five or ten minutes a day—or whatever sits comfortably on your shoulders at this stage. But don't fool yourself or others. There must be integrity in this and no play-acting. Make sure that the importance your mouth attaches to the place of the Quiet Time in your life matches closely its stature in your timetable.

You must realize that growth and maturity, closeness and intimacy do not come in snatches. Three-minute prayers grabbed here and there like a cold hot dog crammed into the mouth between classes doesn't make it. You'll never make any real friends if all you try is an occasional "Hi there" flung across the gym floor. Five minutes of prayer and Bible reading are fine for beginners but if you have been on the pilgrimage for many years, if you intend to put muscles on your skinny Christian frame, then you need to be spending long periods of time alone with your Friend. "When you pray, go into your room, close the door and pray to your Father, who is unseen," said Jesus (Mt. 6:6). Try staying in your room all morning now and then. That's what the great heroes of old have done. Risk a little. Lose some sleep or miss a golf game or two. Spend long times energetically with God. See what happens.

What about Method?

Just as Coles Notes give you a quick handle on such things as Jane Austen's *Pride and Prejudice,* so Bible-reading notes can give you a quick handle on the Scriptures. That might affect your pride and prejudice too. An organization called Scripture Union publishes notes designed specifically for Quiet Times.[3] Their Bible-reading notes cover the range from children to experienced adults and include a plan for reading through the entire Bible in three years. I thoroughly recommend these helps to you as you start your DQT, and they'll last some of you all your lives. One of the most intelligent and respected Christian professors I know, at the University of British Columbia uses the notes daily in her Quiet Time.

Another method is published by InterVarsity Press (let's hear it for the old firm!). Called *This Morning with God,* the series is printed in one volume which takes you through the Bible in four years.[4] For each day there is a short reading followed by half a dozen questions. Unlike the Scripture Union notes, *This Morning with God* does not have a daily comment on the text.

Whatever help you use, the purpose is always the same—get involved with the Scriptures. Become affected by what you read. Assimilate it. Keep a notebook. This is far more serious than jotting down the rambling discourse of a philosophy professor (and how keenly we do that). Note your ideas and responses; check out details you don't understand; keep on asking questions and learn the specific things that God is teaching you out of the daily reading of his Word.

Prayer

The next part of the Quiet Time is prayer. Are you a little disenchanted by it? It's a strange thing, sometimes as boring as yesterday's news, sometimes as difficult as concentration during an after-lunch lecture. At times our prayers are as empty as a discarded Coke can and God as remote as the chance of straight A's. We pray doggedly onward because we know that's what we ought to do.

Yet prayer can be as sweet as the distilled juice of a Mediterranean peach and as exciting as a flight in the cockpit of a Concorde jet. The pacemaker that always brings a new pulse to our prayers is the awareness of Who is on the other end.

Ever been in love? Ever picked up the telephone knowing that the girl or boy of your dreams was at the other end—the one whose voice would momentarily raise your pulse to 120 and bring perspiration to your very kneecaps? You need no encouragement to talk or listen then. It's like this when you are fully aware that it is God at the other end of your prayers. It's not that we are in love with God or foolishly infatuated by a soppy sentimentalism. It's the awesome, mind-stretching realization of who he is that should drop us to our knees like a felled tree. When you know who's calling, you'll come running to the phone.

Pray with a pen and paper in your hand. And if you're going to complain that you can't hold a pen with your hands clasped together and that you can't write with your eyes shut, stick a crayon in your mouth and write on the wallpaper. But write. Make notes of your prayers to him and his messages to you.

Making a Prayer Diary

You can make an organized prayer list. Write down the things and people for whom you wish to pray and put them into seven groups. The number of groups doesn't matter, of course, but I use seven so that I can pray for a different group each day. My groups are organized around such things as family and friends, events of the day and week, and the I-V staff in British Columbia. I am systematically interceding for a variety of people I know, sometimes with definite requests, sometimes with more generalized prayers. And I pray regularly for events that are important.

We have recently begun doing this in our family prayer times also. After breakfast, between the last toast and the mad dash to get the kids on the bus, we take a desk diary and write down the prayer requests from the four of us. We then pray around the table, each one of us taking part. Now I don't want to pretend that we do this every morning, religiously, as you might say. Often we have gotten up too late, or there's an early morning meeting somewhere, or we're just too cranky to open the prayer diary. But there are at least two great advantages to this scheme.

First, it makes our prayers concrete. All four of us are usually praying for something specific to happen as a result of God's involvement. Second, as we look back over the diary each day, checking off the yeses and noes of God's answers, we teach our children and remind ourselves that the Lord answers prayer. "You may ask me for anything in my name, and I will do it," says Jesus in John 14:14. I want us as a family to know that praying has an effect. It changes people, and people change things. Prayer is becoming an indispensable and very normal part of our life together.

You could start your prayer diary even before you go to campus. In six months, you could have enough material to provoke jealousy from old Samuel Pepys, the world's greatest diarist, who kept and published a daily journal of events in seventeenth-century London. You'll have your own version of Acts. You'll have a record of God's patient goodness to you and a history of your spiritual warfare with enough successful skirmishes to keep you going until the final victory is declared.

Keep a section for long-term intercession. This will usually concern healing and conversion, the changing of body and mind. Stay faithful and encouraged. George Mueller prayed for the conversion of six friends. They all eventually became believers although it took twenty years. A friend of mine prayed for seventeen years for the renewal of her husband's faith. It came.

Leave Room for Worship

Finally, leave a place in your DQT for time to worship God. Our prayer times are unbalanced if they are all asking. Tell God that he is worthy. Step back now and then and simply admire.

Some students from a Christian community in Ontario were on a midnight stroll and were suddenly treated to a startling display of the northern lights. They lay on their backs beside the road and stared in admiration. As the show tapered off they broke into spontaneous applause. That's what worship is, a verbal round of applause.

Articulate and celebrate your worship with Scripture. Many of the psalms will put into words your exact feelings of thankfulness and gratitude. "Ascribe to the LORD the glory due his name; worship the LORD in the splendor of his holiness" (Ps. 29:2). Chapters of the book of Revelation, such as four, five, seven and eleven, are tremendous when read aloud. Let the words of Scripture, triumphant in pain, majestic in feebleness, victorious in defeat, lift your heart and mind to the very throne of the King. Sing, play music, read and recite. Find that special place on the beach or walk on the cliffs in the howling wind. Lift your head and cry aloud with all the saints of all ages and all times, "Worthy is the Lamb, who was slain, to receive power and wealth and wisdom and strength and honor and glory and praise" (Rev. 5:12).

Suggested reading:
White, John. "Prayer" and "God Still Speaks," chapters 2 and 3 of *The Fight.* Downers Grove, Ill.: InterVarsity Press, 1976.
Quiet Time. Downers Grove, Ill.: InterVarsity Press, 1976.
White, John. *Daring to Draw Near: People in Prayer.* Downers Grove, Ill.: InterVarsity Press, 1977.

4

Big Bad Profs

My wife is a microbiologist, a very impressive fact that I like
to drop casually at parties. She once worked as a teaching assistant at a university in western Canada. After final exams,
during the marking, she watched in dismay and anger as one
of the professors raised certain students' grades to A's, in some
cases because they were friends of his daughter or in one case
because she had been the pretty Engineers' Queen. This goes
to prove something you are rapidly learning in your first term
—some professors are nasty.

Traditionally, our society has held certain people in awe:
judges and lawyers, for example, and doctors. To have learned
that a respected lawyer or a prominent politician was involved
in corruption or immorality or had been foolish or negligent
would have shocked us fifty years ago. Nowadays, imbued with
cynicism, we are barely dismayed when a high court judge is
suspended for his drunken involvement with a prostitute, as
happened in Vancouver.

University faculty are included in that special group of pro-
fessionals who are held in awe by the general population. It is

a high distinction to be a university professor, and rightly so. We tend, however, to make two mistakes about this elite group: we think that they are all perfectly sound, well-rounded, nicely balanced individuals, and we assume that they never make mistakes and are consequently beyond criticism. It will take you three days in your first five courses for you to discover that not all university professors measure up.

The revolution of the sixties and the spirit of our iconoclastic age have helped us to dethrone these idols to a degree. But a timid first-year student, cowering under the threat of tutorial vengeance, finds it very difficult to do anything about a genuinely bad professor.

When Professors Eat Students for Breakfast
I'm not concerned in this chapter with profs who are boring or

dull or academically incompetent. You can usually trade courses or sections or get out of the class somehow. Reading the student handbook may forewarn you of such people. I would certainly encourage you to get into good teachers' classes whenever possible. They are the greatest intellectual gift the university has to offer, like a baron of beef smorgasbord after carrot sticks and celery juice. For next semester get some prior information about the teachers. It is no fun and it can be academically demoralizing to sit with a dud for a whole term. My concern in this chapter, however, is with those professors who are running roughshod over the faith, emotions and personalities of certain students, who are doing harm in a savage and direct way.

The teaching profession is, I suppose, like any other large profession in the Western world. It attracts the whole gamut of psychological and emotional types. There are a few of these whose personality and character make them unfit to be in charge of a classroom. They genuinely hurt students; they sneer and mock; they gain their own superiority at the expense of everyone else's dignity. So this chapter is addressed to students who have found themselves in a cage with a tiger.

The essence of this type of crushing assault is that the professor attacks virulently one or two particular targets—often the student herself or himself, sometimes the Christian faith that a student brightly reveals in the classroom.

Some very sad cases of mistreatment have come my way in the past four years. Fortunately, not many. I should say, and I do so happily and thankfully, that the vast majority of professors are fine, outstanding men and women who have a genuine care for their students. But now and then, I've met a prof who loves to trample all over the class. A student's long hours of applied study resulting in a weighty paper have been neutralized by a scorching attack on the writer. Tentative answers to in-class questions have been scorned and ridiculed. Simple questions from the floor have been crumpled up and hurled into the wastebasket as being absurd. Students have had to endure foul language and

obscene jokes, made worse by the enthusiastic reception given
them by members of the class who egg on the trendy prof's
attempts to be modern. Many followers of Jesus have winced as
their Lord and their beliefs are decried and defamed. What can
you do in situations like these?

Courage to Confront

A basic principle holds good in this difficulty as it does in all—
share it. Talk to your closest friends; share your anguish with
some Christian students and let other students in your class
know how you feel about the continual barrage from the black-
board. You'll pick up unexpected support this way. Yet at the
same time, keep it private among a select few. I am not recom-
mending that you gossip your complaint all around campus.

My wife, while happy with her French professor's desire to
enliven his teaching with songs and films, was depressed by his
continual use of media that was sexually explicit and titillating.
The four-letter word is the same in most languages, and while
doing nothing to improve her French its continued use became
increasingly offensive. She shared her concerns with a classmate
one day and got this response: "Oh, I'm so glad you mentioned
that. It offends me too but I was too scared to say anything."

This problem of fear keeps most of us with our mouths firmly
closed. We are afraid, and understandably so. None of us likes
confrontation and argument, and none of us is eager to endure
the sort of revenge that might come our way. But to encourage
you, I'll tell you the rest of the story about Elaine's French class.
She went to see the prof—not without apprehension—and ex-
plained carefully and politely to him that she found the amount
of sexual material and the number of obscenities in his class to
be offensive. She did not rail at him; there was no rancor in
her tone, and she did not preach the gospel to him either. She
simply stated her case. The professor thanked her for her comments and received her criticism with equal politeness. Though
he defended himself and attempted to justify his selection of ma-

terial, he promised her that he would change his tack. And he did. There was a noticeable decrease in the offensive material.

Several other students were delighted at the change in the tone of the class, and although Elaine was a marked woman from then on, receiving ominous and meaningful stares whenever there was the mention of sex or the use of a swear word, she did not suffer in any other way. In fact, she thinks that she probably gained in the estimation and respect of the teacher. She certainly had been true to herself and to what she saw as the will of God.

Two points surface right away: it is possible to effect change, number one; but it will take courage, number two. For those who wish courageously to work to effect change . . . read on.

Using the System as Defense

There are two lines of defense in this area of teacher abuse, exploitation, unfairness or attack. The first line of defense is to go through the official university procedures, availing yourself of such people as the ombudsperson, the dean or the student union representatives. The second line of defense is to use the people of the kingdom, wearing the armor of God and bringing the Spirit of God into the action. You might not necessarily have to choose between one line of defense or the other; you could happily pursue both.

For most situations, the first person to tackle is undoubtedly the offending professor. This is a difficult interview to face, and it always appears easier to complain to a third party first. But taking your complaint to someone other than the professor first is unfair and deceitful; so avoid the temptation to take the easy way out at the start. If there is no receptivity by your teacher, then I would see that the way is clear to follow the grievance procedures provided.

Start by getting some information from the student union people. What are the grievance procedures on campus? How do you file a complaint? Has this particular professor any history of such things? Is she always hostile to Christians? Has he propositioned or molested anyone before? Be careful now. If you are to complain officially about the behavior of a member of the university faculty or staff, your own behavior must be a model of politeness and respect. It's no good to burst ranting and raving into the dean's office.

There is a Christian way to follow a grievance procedure, and even though you may be angry or humiliated, try to remain polite. The quiet voice of insistent reason speaks far louder than the apoplectic ranting of temper. "Reckless words pierce like a sword, but the tongue of the wise brings healing" (Prov. 12:18). If healing, rather than compensation is the Christian's objective, gentle, reserved, polite speech will be the means.

The astounding words of Jesus in Matthew 5 teach us what our attitude should be toward those whom we have to confront. "Love your enemies and pray for those who persecute you" (v. 44). That sour professor of chemistry whose sarcasm is destroying you is still a person, commanding respect like all people by virtue of being loved by God.

When you file your complaint, you must not be unprepared. Document your case. Write down the facts and have witnesses to the words and events. Scrupulous honesty and fairness are to be the hallmark of your report. So neither overstate your case with emotional hyperbole nor back off from the truth. Be discreet but firm. You have nothing to lose but your grades.

Using God's People as Defense

The second line of defense starts within the context of your Christian minicommunity. Gather round you your small group members or a half-dozen other Christians you can trust. Let them know the problem but ask them to keep it to themselves. You need to take sensible precautions against gossip and wild rumors. Keep the whole thing containable. Please don't get up in front of your entire Christian fellowship and tell them that Professor Paramecium keeps putting his hand on your knee as you peer through the microscope together during botany labs. One great relief of sharing with your Christian friends is that it now becomes their problem too, and in the encouragement of prayer and problem sharing the weight of the burden on your own lone shoulders is considerably lightened.

Your friends can also help you throw an objective light on the situation and to look at the problem through the biblical lens.

When to Defend

The agonizing question in these affairs is whether to do something or not. Do we blow the whistle? Should we tell? Ought we to complain? The guidelines come from the Bible.

There is no biblical mandate to act out of peevishness; there is no nice Christian way to get your own back; and there are no spiritual techniques for restoring your damaged pride. But there is an overwhelming biblical case for seeking justice and practicing righteousness. "Hate evil, and love good, and establish justice in the gate.... Let justice roll down like waters, and righteousness like an everflowing stream" (Amos 5:15, 24 RSV). If your complaint serves the cause of justice, if it is biblically right, then God's command is to expose the evil.

Paul's advice to speak the truth in love (Eph. 4:15) certainly gives us the correct attitude. It is still starkly clear, though, that we ought to be "speaking the truth."

If you feel that registering the complaint is right in line with the voice of the Old Testament calling for justice and righteousness, if you believe that you are under obligation to speak the truth in love, then you may set the wheels in motion knowing that you have a biblical mandate to act and are not merely serving your own selfish ends.

Another gift the Christian community offers in support is knowing that as you sit painfully through another hour of humiliation and ridicule or as you knock tremblingly on the teacher's door to confront him or her, there are six hulking

Christians in the room next door praying for you. Prayer brings its own comfort; so does the affirmation that God hears and is already involved in the situation to protect you and see you through. That's part of his commitment to you.

I met two instances last year in which emotionally damaged students were helped in these ways. In both cases, the students were having their work ridiculed. Worse than the series of D's at the bottom of the page were the scornful comments, the scorching sarcasm in class discussions and the relentless put-downs. It's hard to hang on to your dignity and humanity when you are constantly being told that you should repeat kindergarten.

So these two students shared their problems with me and their student friends and built up a small group for support and advice. The advice was, "Do something about it. It's serious, extraordinary and unwarranted. It's affecting the whole class, and you need to speak on their behalf too. Take the lead and risk it. We believe there is biblical justification for your action."

After reflection and considerable prayer, each of the abused students went to their teachers. The response by the teachers differed, but both of them listened and obviously respected the students for what they were doing. There were noticeable differences in their behavior afterward, although the classroom was not turned overnight into a Buckingham Palace garden party.

If you decide to confront the teacher, it is probably wise to go by yourself or at least with only one or two others who are affected. It is very tempting to take with you your entire campus fellowship or at least those who play on the rugby team (thirty-five enormous Christians, all very large, are persuasive), but they can't help you. You do not want to put your instructor on the defensive by a pretense of intimidation.

One interesting sidelight on all this is that the two students who spoke to their teachers gained some valuable insights into the reasons why their teachers were behaving so extraordinarily.

It is often very sobering to discover some of the details of a teacher's private life. There might be death and disease, divorce and separation, despair and depression. There are usually good causes of bad behavior.

A Tough Skin Helps

Lastly, prepare to be a bit tough-skinned on this issue. Only the extremes of verbal assault call for action. You'll hear a lot of dirty jokes by trendy professors in your four years; you'll hear a lot of obscenity and foul language; your literature classes will be reading pornographic books and your drama group will go to dirty movies. That is simply part and parcel of being a student on a secular campus, and you need to realize the contemporary morality out of which all this stuff comes. Grin and bear most of it; you're in it for the next four years.

Try not to take it too personally or get all upset when your history professor lays all the blame for the woes of the last two thousand years at the feet of the Christian church, though in an appropriate way you might like to challenge him or her on that generalization. Remember that class essays are not really the place to attack professors or state the six easy steps for spiritual peace or even to quote John 3:16. You must get all this into perspective. Your teachers may include atheists and Marxists, existentialists and humanists, meditators and addicts.

Christian dignity still lives even when you must listen to what humanist teachers presuppose about the nature of humanity, even when you are learning what amoral teachers think about the glories of promiscuity. Atheistic presuppositions and immoral lifestyles do not have to be instantly and loudly refuted for you to remain true to the "faith once and for all delivered to the saints."

Later, probably in upper-class courses and advanced seminars, you can pursue the exciting chase of hunting and identifying presuppositions and exposing the hollowness of non-Christian world views. There is literature to help you.[5] But there is no shame involved, and you are not denying the lordship of Jesus if you have to write a Freudian analysis of a D. H. Lawrence novel or chart the timetable for the evolution of the universe. In the academic world, wear your faith lightly sometimes. Don't always rise to the bait. Know that all truth is in Christ Jesus and nothing can hurt that. Rest your case.

Suggested reading:
Alexander, John W. *Practical Criticism: Giving It and Taking It.* Downers Grove, Ill.: InterVarsity Press, 1976.
Augsburger, David. *Caring Enough to Confront.* Glendale, Calif.: Regal Books, 1973.

5

Men's and Women's
Sana in Corpore Sano

It seems that back in the good old days of the little store on Main Street, there were in fact two little stores on Main Street, both of which were specialist sellers of sports equipment. Being side by side, they were intensely competitive and nowhere was the competition more obvious than in their rival advertising. As soon as one store put up an advertisement, the other store tried to top it.

So "Grand Sale" in one store quickly became "Grand Giveaway Sale" in the other, and as one store started off with "Add a little outdoors to your life" so the other topped it with "Our indoors can add more outdoors to your life." And the rivalry continued.

Eventually, one store got the clever idea of using the famous Latin motto "Mens Sana in Corpore Sano" which means "A Healthy Mind in a Healthy Body." This saying is the intellectual motto for educated athletes and outdoorspeople. The competition next door, never to be outdone, but not knowing what the strange words meant, topped the advertisement by adding: "Men's and Women's Sana in Corpore Sano."

All this is a catchy introduction to the topic of this chapter—wholeness.

The Wholistic Lifestyle

One of the things that Inter-Varsity student groups have taught me in the last four years is that God calls us to a wholistic life-style, that God is interested in redeeming the total person and working out what that means in all life's activities. Students have often shown a healthy disregard for that spurious division between the sacred and the secular. I distinctly remember going to a stage performance of Woody Herman's Jazz Band and being so impressed and delighted by it that as I left I prayed and thanked God for such a tremendous experience. That's an example of wholistic thinking. We don't just thank God for Christian music; we thank him for music. Period.

Christians are people who are trying to develop healthy minds in their healthy bodies. Now our minds and bodies are not healthy in the sense that they are perfect, beautiful and flawless. They are healthy in the sense that they clearly fulfill the purposes for which they were designed. Christians are just trying to follow the Maker's instructions and keep the warranty in effect.

To be a follower of Jesus is to be neither a pale, bland, colorless and odorless ascetic, denying all pleasures of the flesh, nor to be a paunchy, touchy-feely blob of sensuous sentimentality denying any discipline or rigor of the mind. God has redeemed us entirely, body, soul, mind, spirit and emotions, and as such expects us to live with balance and harmony in this fractured and distorted world.

Deuteronomy 6:4 is an Old Testament call for us to respond wholly to God. "Hear, O Israel: The LORD our God is one LORD; and you shall love the LORD your God with all your heart, and with all your soul, and with all your might" (RSV). With the heart we give to God our feelings; with the soul we give to God our will; with might we give to God our fierce energy. All these qualities are riveted on the living God, who, like a mirror, reflects the picture of his total commitment to us.

A New Testament reference to wholism is found in John 10:10, where Jesus says, "I have come that they may have life, and have it to the full." There is never the sense that God is wanting to cut life down to bite-sized chunks or shave off the better parts for himself. God, who is the very author of every idea in the cosmos from daffodils to hang gliding, who is the very essence of imagination, wants to involve us in the great adventure called Life because that's what we were designed for.

You and "Them"
What does this mean for the university student going to campus for the first time? Well, I want to give you a negative warning and a positive encouragement. The warning is: do not be afraid of "them." The encouragement is: explore all the varied ways in which you can become truly you.

Who are "them"? Or, to be a little more grammatical for all you language majors, who are "they"? They are anyone who is not "one of us": big, hairy football players who crunch people like celery, singing foul songs and swilling beer as they go; trendy artistic and musical types, oozing the laid-back lifestyle through their faded jeans and dark glasses; eager junior nuclear scientists doodling diagrams of plutonium bombs on the backs of old copies of *Scientific American;* blond titans of the Ski Club, male and female, cloned copies of *Cosmopolitan* and Air Canada models, dripping sexuality; bearded philosophers in sandals and ex-DND greatcoats, graduates of the Katmandu drug pilgrimage and Erhardt Training Seminars, preaching anarchy.

They do, admittedly, look terrifying. They all seem to be so confident, so loud, so authoritative, so dynamic. Some of them are, I suppose. But many of them are lonely and insecure, uncertain in their brashness and isolated in their promiscuity. Whoever they are and whatever they are, don't let them frighten you from joining their activities. Sign up for the University

Though they may look different, some of "them" are just like you.

Chorus and the Campus Players; try out for the football team and go on the Ski Club trip; be a leader in the Philosophy Society and join the Committee for a Nuclear-Powered Model Railway. Part of your freedom as a person and your task as a Christian is to get involved, to go where people are, to be with students in all their activities and situations, as long as the ethics of the kingdom of God are not disobeyed.

How Could Jesus Do Such a Thing?

Jesus showed this freedom as he fulfilled his task on earth. Involvement was part and parcel of his strategy of getting close to people and changing them. He went to all sorts of places, including some of the worst. ("Did you hear? He's gone to Levi's house and everybody knows that Levi is the greediest legal thief this side of Rome!") He talked to all sorts of people, including the very worst. ("Have you heard the latest? He's gone to that snob Simon's house now, for supper. And he talked for hours to a whore!") He met sinners, talked to them, dined with them and changed them. They loved him for it while some of his friends became his enemies because of it. He lived this type of lifestyle without ever compromising his position as God incarnate or forsaking his pledged obedience to his Father. How could he do it?

He could do it, first, because he knew exactly who he was and where his identity and security came from. Only when you know who you are can you be free to take up the towel and wash people's feet. "Jesus knew that the Father had put all things under his power, and that he had come from God and was returning to God" (Jn. 13:3). Most of us are so insecure, so perplexed about our identity, that we hang on grimly to all sorts of status symbols to make it appear that we have a vestige of goodness. We're fearful, reluctant to associate with the majority of students lest our righteousness be compromised.

Second, Jesus safeguarded his own ethic and was refreshingly unjudgmental about the behavior of others. That doesn't mean he accepted it all; it means that he left judgment to another person, another place and another time (Jn. 8:1-11). Determinedly hanging on to his own standards of honesty and integrity, he was never persuaded to quit the faith and become like the people who surrounded him. If you are safe on those two bases, identity and ethics, you are ready to play ball with the rest of the campus.

The purpose in all this is that you, a member of the church

of Christ Jesus at your university, can become the cutting edge
of evangelism. But how on earth can Christians be the cutting
edge of the church if the scissors and cloth never come into
contact? So many of us are sharpened blades cutting through
swaths of empty air.

Contact is the key that opens up the door to communication.
The grand purpose of all this mingling with the sweat of humanity, this playing and working with "them," is to bring the
salt and light to the very places where there is putrefaction
and darkness. Don't hide in the shaker or the cellar. Please come
out.

Going back to the metaphor of chapter one, we are all part
of an artful Christian plot to spread light throughout the darkness of enemy territory. And the only way we can do that is by
penetration and involvement.

So don't let them scare you off—join them.

Find Out Who You Are
University is, of all times and places, the best to explore and
discover your own gifts and interests. The most fascinating
clubs and societies abound on North American campuses. Give
yourself room to investigate and grow; you're going to become a
different person from the one you were at high school. You
might find out that you're intrigued by falconry. Hurray! The
world needs more Christian falconers.

Ralph and Sandi were two Christian students at the University of Victoria who wanted to do a sport together, just to relax
and keep fit. They chose rowing. Now, both of them have won
gold medals at the national level and have brought some evangelistic salt and light into the rowing community.

Andrea entered debating during her first year, and nearly
convinced the Student Union Vice President, her constant debate
adversary, to become a Christian by the end of spring term. The
happiest, most fulfilled Christian students I know are the ones
who are heavily involved in all sorts of campus activities.

Signing Up

In the flurry of Clubs' Day excitement and propaganda, in the new enthusiasm of being a university student at last with its exposure to all things bright and beautiful (and not so), it is very tempting to sign up for sixteen clubs, try out for five teams and see if anyone else is interested in translating the *Guinness Book of World Records* into Urdu (just to get your name in the book, of course). But I want to caution you against overexposure.

Such extended involvement only works at the expense of your studies. Eventually you'll find out that you have to drop your five courses to have enough time to keep up with your recreational load.

Hear these seasoned words of wisdom: you must give priority to your studies. My experience with student life is that it is very difficult to either enjoy or be good at extracurricular stuff, including your Christian fellowship, if you are behind in your assignments or flunking a course or two. A reasoned look at your calendar will help you decide just how much time you can spend with the Troglodite Club without its being detrimental to your studies.

Remember, too, that the Lord of your personal devotions is also the Lord of the Fencing Club. Just as he wishes to guide you and use you as a disciple, so he wishes to guide you and use you as a fencer. It's all part of his world. So allow yourself to be directed by him; lay your ideas about campus involvement in front of him and ask for help in deciding where to sign up. "I will instruct you and teach you in the way you should go" (Ps. 32:8). Look ahead a little, too. The Ski Club may not take very much of your time in September and October but what about January and February, just before midterms? Watch those weekends.

Conflicts of Interest

All this deciding and signing-up is not going to be very easy for you, and the more you are interested in life and in people the more difficult it becomes. There's an irony there. As God leads you energetically into the big world around you, it becomes harder to cope with the problem of time and commitments.

Facing you squarely during the first month on campus is the problem of priorities. What do you do when you find that the Scuba Club conflicts with your campus fellowship? What happens if one of the campus clubs, clamoring for leadership as they all are, pressures you to join their executive when Inter-Varsity has invited you to be a Bible study leader? Should you let the Chess Club seduce you or not?

I'll offer two guidelines. There is a hierarchy of values, at the level of principle and at the level of specifics, which states that some things are more important than others. If I am given the stark choice between visiting a dying friend injured in a road accident and flying to Miami for a weekend jaunt with the marine biology dilettantes, I must choose the former. It's clearly more important for me to comfort and minister to my dying friend than to go beachcombing in the southern sunshine.

But rarely is the choice as simple or as stark as that one. Let's attack the problem at the level of principle first.

A Hierarchy of Principles
In principle, it is always more important to be involved in service than in pleasure. If I am trying to choose between two activities that extend over a long period of time, I can ask this question: in principle, which of the two activities will enhance my service as a Christian disciple and increase my usefulness as a member of God's kingdom? For example, is it better to spend eight weekends improving my ability as a skier or to spend those days organizing activities at a downtown youth center?

The principle in this example is clear. It is better to do the thing that will strengthen you as a follower of Jesus, and your spiritual strength will develop more in the youth center gym than the après-ski bar.

The aim of our lives is to grow to be like Christ and to accept commitments that shape us in his image is to choose sensibly and well. Over the long haul, all the luggage we carry must be labeled for the same destination. We can change our method of transportation, but everything we carry must have an identical tag.

Gary had to stop playing drums with a local jazz combo because he discovered that this particular suitcase had the wrong label. There were just too many Sunday engagements and too many drinks between songs. In principle, he knew that the jazz group was leading him away from God.

Exceptions

It is harder to write advice with regard to decision making at the level of specifics rather than principles. Although no Christian would ever say that, in principle, going skiing is more important than going to church, there are obviously occasions on which it is legitimate to miss church and go skiing. Or to miss the Bible study and go for a jog with a friend.

I don't want to dress this up in some sort of superspirituality. I've heard too much syrupy talk of how righteous it is to play tennis on Sunday morning as long as you're evangelizing the players as you do so. My point is that it's all right to go off and play tennis purely for your own enjoyment. To go skiing with a good friend, to spend Sunday with your non-Christian roommate or to cheer a lonely international student by playing tour guide are fine ways to spend time, in and of themselves.

It is also perfectly legal to miss a particular Christian meeting for your own sake, just because you need the rest, the change or the relaxation. I've often thought—quietly, though, for I don't know if such thoughts are allowed—that some Christian students go to too many Christian meetings. I almost long for some of them to go somewhere else, anywhere else, where they can build into their lives some of the balance of the wholistic life.

Noticing that David, an excellent student leader in the Inter-Varsity chapter where I was a staff worker, was looking exhausted, I sat down with him and asked him to draw up a list of all the commitments he had in the forthcoming week. To our amazement and horror, he had fifteen Christian meetings and appointments that week. No wonder the imbalance of his lifestyle was showing in his pale face and tired eyes. Grimly, we took the blue pencil in hand and censored half of his meetings.

That wasn't particularly easy. Should he cancel his coffee appointment with Joan, who was in need of the real friendship and understanding David could offer? Should he not meet with the Work Day committee? Should he cancel his breakfast prayer group?

Frankly, there will be times when neither you nor anyone else knows how to make the decision of how you are going to solve any particular conflict. Such decisions are complicated and difficult. But Dave and I worked at it using the criteria I mentioned: which engagements were helping him grow in his Christian walk and which appointments were once-only deals that could be treated at the level of specifics? Then, when the choices were clearly focused, it became easier to decide which were the more important and valuable.

You can be assured by the fact that God is the Lord of all choices, more eager to guide you than you are to be led. Take heart and listen to his voice. "Whether you turn to the right or to the left, your ears will hear a voice behind you, saying, 'This is the way; walk in it' " (Is. 30:21).

Prune Back All Round

If you find that you are being choked to death by too many activities and responsibilities, you need to break free before your commitments throttle you. But as you chop back the tentacles around your throat, as you hack away at the limbs and branches twisting their way around your neck, do a general prune. Cut back some branches here and some limbs over there, letting the sun shine in from all sides and the wind blow cleanly through.

Above all, maintain that sense of balance between specifically religious involvements (like going to meetings) and the rest of your activities.

I was recently leaning over a painted plywood wall in Vancouver watching with wonder the activity at a huge building site. The tall tower crane fascinated me most. In the strong wind blowing straight in from the Pacific, the thin spidery creation was swaying alarmingly on its slender pedestal. How could it stay upright?

The crane remains erect because the whole thing is balanced. The long girder that reaches out over the construction site and carries the actual lifting apparatus is cleverly balanced by enormous slabs of concrete tucked away under the framework on the opposite side. Without that counterweight, the crane will tip over and collapse.

The crane is a perfect image of what I am trying to talk about when I plead for a balance in your Christian lives. I want believing students to have both the long, horizontal reach into the unbelieving world and the slabs of Christian fellowship for balance. To stay in balance means adding fellowship weight in proportion to extending evangelistic outreach, increasing the weight of concrete as you extend the metal lifting arm. To prune back one side of the fulcrum you must prune back the other if you wish to stay balanced.

You could actually draw a picture of your wholistic lifestyle using the tower crane as an image. Along the horizontal arm you could write in all the various involvements you have with people and events around you, on campus and in your community. On the other side, you could write down all your specifically Christian commitments—your Bible studies and prayer groups.

If the picture shows you that you are far too busy, take off equally from both sides. If you want to increase your involvements, add equally. But whatever you do, don't topple over.

Suggested reading:
Stott, John R. W. *Balanced Christianity.* Downers Grove, Ill.: InterVarsity Press, 1975.
Hummel, Charles E. *Tyranny of the Urgent.* Downers Grove, Ill.: InterVarsity Press, 1967.
Alexander, John W. *Managing Our Work.* Downers Grove, Ill.: InterVarsity Press, 1975.

6

"Come into My Tent"

The sinister voice of the devil filled the courtyard as he commissioned his agent Lust on her mission of seek and seduce. His scarlet coat shone in the sunlight, his sleek, black beard pointed toward the sky as he threw back his horned head and laughed diabolically. Lust adjusted the balloons in her bosom, patted her hair into shape and sashayed off on her conquest.

I was watching a performance of *The Hound of Everyman* played by a traveling troupe called "The Lamb's Players." The setting was Market Square in Victoria, ideally suited to a medieval drama, with its courtyard of brick and stone, wooden benches and rustic balcony.

This updated version of the Everyman classic is extremely funny. The hero runs into a whole series of stylized temptations, characters commissioned by the devil to tempt Everyman away from his journey toward belief in God. Lust and Drunkenness were easy to act; the lures of pseudointellectualism and crystal-ball spiritualism less so.

It was very satisfying to be able to watch and clearly identify each trap as it was set. We all joined in the spirit of the play, cheering the hero each time he gained a victory, moaning at defeats and energetically booing each successive tempter. It reminded me of an advertisement I had seen at a movie theatre in Lagos, Nigeria.

The advertisement showed a comparison between clothes washed in Tide and those washed in Brand X. When the grayish clothes were being shown, the audience booed. When the housewife came back with a packet of Tide, everyone broke into cheers and stomped their feet.

Cheering for Tide and booing Pride are fun. Clichés of seduction, like the desert beauty whispering "come into my tent," are Turkish delights to us. But when we see that, as in the play, Satan and Death are always lurking behind the shoulders of each tempter, we begin to see the point and sober up a bit.

Recognizing Temptation

I've often thought it would be much easier if temptation were as simple to identify in real life as it was in that stage play. If Lust were always a vamp, at least it would be easy to recognize her—though it still might be difficult to send her on her way.

I don't want to give the impression that sex is the only temptation or the worst. There are lots of temptations stashed away in the tempter's closet, waiting to be brought out in a dazzling array of tawdry beauty as you trip your way to prayer meeting. It will help us if we can unmask some of these beauties and establish a strategy for dealing with them. For temptations must be dealt with; they must be conquered. That's in your contract with the Savior.

Most temptations will strike you in the area of bodily appetites and sensuality. It is a great temptation to be lazy, especially at 7:30 A.M. on a day of freezing rain in Calgary when the softness of the sheets compares favorably to old Dozo and his 8:00 class on bugs. It's tempting to be slothful, to pamper and spoil the body. And it's tempting just to sit around and eat too much or drink too much or spend hours gazing fondly into the mirror at your shoulder-length blonde hair.

Temptations will hit you in the arena of your mind too: in the pride of academic achievement or in the superiority of elitism; in the excellence of your mind and the speed of your wit (as if you had anything to do with that). Or you will be tempted to think that your own particular brand of scriptural understanding is the last word on truth, or you will find yourself slowly justifying your flirt with humanism and unbelief.

Knowing, however, that the root of all temptation is in the spiritual warfare between God and his enemy, there will be temptations for you in the realm of your spirit. Satan will actively try to lure your soul out of the kingdom of light into the cells of darkness. The Enemy will creep silently up to your ear and whisper his favorite opening gambit, "Did God say . . . ?" And he will sow doubts—doubts about your conversion, doubts about your holiness and doubts about your growth.

What Temptation Is and Isn't

It's time to identify what a temptation is—not temptation in general, but the definite specific temptations that jump out from the corner. A temptation is always an invitation for you to make a wrong choice. That choice is wrong because it gets you to do something, follow a course of action or develop a set of attitudes that will lead you momentarily, or for longer, away from God's design for your life.

A summary of God's design for you is found in John 15:16. "I chose you to go and bear fruit—fruit that will last." Temptation attacks the fruitfulness. It encourages you to choose things that prevent your development into Christlikeness. It wants to destroy all your biblical qualities. Temptation is to your fruitfulness as a cutworm to a watermelon.

Although some temptations are very subtle, leading you circuitously down gray alleys of diversion where moral signposts have fallen and been effaced, much temptation is simply an open invitation to sin.

Don't fool yourself about real sin. All sorts of lifestyles are on display around you, including hedonistic forms of liberalized Christianity that seem to be a common-law marriage between *Hustler* and HIS. An invitation to sin, overt and bald, is easily recognized and must be instantly rejected. There's no discussion about whether it's a temptation or not to tell a lie or be disloyal or sleep around. The guidelines are clearly drawn up in Scripture.

"The acts of the sinful nature are obvious: sexual immorality, impurity and debauchery; idolatry and witchcraft; hatred, discord, jealousy, fits of rage, selfish ambition, dissensions, factions and envy; drunkenness, orgies, and the like. I warn you, as I did before, that those who live like this will not inherit the kingdom of God" (Gal. 5:19-21). That's not a hypothesis for debate. That is the revealed judgment of God.

Temptation, then, is always an invitation. And as with all other invitations, it must be accepted or rejected.

Please understand, though, that receiving the invitation is not wrong. It is not sin to be tempted, for Jesus himself was tempted in everything, "just as we are" (Heb. 4:15). The bonus of this similarity between us and Jesus is that he is able to help us because he knows what it's like. "Because he himself suffered when he was tempted, he is able to help those who are being tempted" (Heb. 2:18).

The task of identifying the things that are uniquely your temptations boils down to one question. What are the invitations coming your way that will lure you from the serious business of developing a fruitful life according to the pattern established by Jesus?

Yielding

I want to free you from the errors of hypersensitivity and over-scrupulousness. (That means I don't want you to be a prig.) Many Christians are so sensitive to temptation that they think any instance of luxury, any moment of ease, any minute of indulgence or "worldliness" is akin to being wrenched off the straight and narrow and hurled onto the express lane to Pitland. I believe that taking the extra doughnut, enjoying a huge meal at a good restaurant, sleeping in for one long, lazy morning, buying yourself a gift just because it isn't your birthday, skipping class to go canoeing or getting an Afro haircut can be healthy, normal, God-given moments of fun and enjoyment. I'm sure that God, author of fun, maker of wine, inventor of sleep, does not wish us to go through life with the ironclad determination to resist and refuse every single moment of pleasure. So feel free to enjoy food and rest, music and entertainment, surprise gifts and unexpected holidays, for such is your right as a child of freedom.

Where you need to be alert and strong is in the area of quantity. How many times are you choosing ease and comfort? When the occasional choice to do something frivolous is slowly becoming the habitual choice, you might be getting into trouble. It's all right to accept an occasional invitation to a party, but if you accept party invitations day after day you are obviously making decisions that will begin to take you away from the disciplined life of a follower of Jesus. Continual partying pushes out room for anything else. When you have bought yourself the third surprise gift in three days, or when you find yourself haunting the cafeteria line-ups for seconds and thirds at every meal, or when you have stayed late in bed for the fourth day running, then you must blow the whistle on yourself and ask if these choices are not actually becoming sins.

Here is the basic issue. Every time you make a decision to accept or reject an invitation, you are putting another brick into the wall of your character. Your life adds up to the sum total of your decisions. Every choice you make now affects the way in which you make all choices, building your life upward in the shape of Christlike discipleship or eroding the foundations of faith so that eventually your house falls. To find that you are giving in more and more often to the impulse to buy some new addition to your wardrobe is to find that your whole sense of values is taking on a warped shape, a shape that says buying clothes for yourself is of prime importance. You should be uncomfortable with that.

The temptation scale, then, may run something like this. One special surprise new shirt or blouse a year—no temptation. You have not succumbed to galloping sartorial disease. You are not establishing a pattern of behavior that is going to place an inordinate value on the pleasure and need of clothes.

Two or three surprise shirts a term? Some anxiety. That's a lot of money to be spending on clothes when there is so great a need around you, and you know the biblical call to be a good steward. It suggests an emphasis on the importance of clothes that is in discord with the values of the kingdom and their emphasis on the inner nature. "Your beauty should not come from outward adornment, such as braided hair and the wearing of gold jewelry and fine clothes. Instead, it should be that of your inner self, the unfading beauty of a gentle and quiet spirit, which is of great worth in God's sight" (1 Pet. 3:3).

If you find that you are buying yourself new clothes each month, then you are obviously in trouble. You are becoming selfish and a slave to fashion. You are being tempted to indulge yourself, and you are yielding to the temptation. Cut your credit card in half and wear the same two pairs of jeans for the rest of the year.

Fighting the Urge
Some temptations are of extraordinary power. Their power comes from the fact that you are particularly weak in that one area. Rather than flirting with some sort of compromise solution, abstain. If, for example, you are tempted to own every jazz record that has ever been put out and you can't walk into a record store without your feet automatically syncopating their way over to the new jazz albums, then quit buying records altogether. Beg, borrow or ban them. Don't buy.

Sometimes, the temptation is so extraordinarily powerful that the only sensible thing to do is run away. I remember a student who had great difficulty in keeping his eyes off the window display of a couple of adult bookstores. No matter how hard he battled to stare straight ahead, he found that his eyes were magnetically pulled toward the naked women on the front covers. He fought a depressing and losing battle with his eyes day after day because those two stores were right on his daily walk to campus. We talked together about his problem and came up with a great solution. He needed to find a new way to the university.

We got a map and drew an alternative route that would avoid both of those stores. So now the fight was removed from his eyes to his feet. But he had far greater control over his feet than his eyes, so he won this particular round. "But you, man of God, flee from all this, and pursue righteousness," Paul advises Timothy twice in his letters (1 Tim. 6:11; 2 Tim. 2:22). If necessary, then, run away.

I remember when I was a cadet at sea school that I was put in the boxing ring to learn the nobler arts of pugilism. Being a somewhat skinny youth, who has since grown into a somewhat skinny man, I climbed into the ring with more than a little apprehension. Fighting with a good friend of mine, a stocky, tougher kid, I was happy to have stayed on my feet for two rounds. Then, halfway through the last round, I saw what was obviously the beginning of a punch that was going to lift my head off my shoulders and bring my nautical career and probably my life to a short, bitter end. The punch, one of those swinging, amateur right-handers, started low, about two inches off the canvas, and climbed at the speed of light toward my chin. I did what any sane man would have done in my position. I turned my back and ran for my corner. Actually, that was the cleverest thing I could have done. Everybody applauded me, even my friendly opponent, saying that if the punch had landed I would never have seen the light of day again.

Therefore, my friends, when you recognize temptation coming straight at you, and coming on strong, turn and run away.

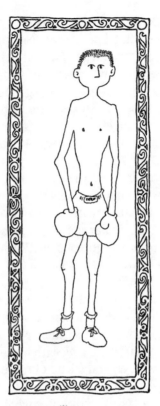

Portrait of the author as a young pugilist

Flee. There's no shame in running, and you'll be accompanied by the cheers of the saints congratulating your common sense. The most spiritual part of your body might well be your legs. In 1 Corinthians 10:13 Paul writes, "God ... will not let you be tempted beyond what you can bear. But when you are tempted, he will also provide a way out so that you can stand up under it." Your legs could be your exit.

Temptation often gains its power the longer you stare at it. In fact, temptation is designed with just that sort of visual appeal: The more you look at it, the more attractive it becomes. David knew he was looking right at temptation when he spotted Bathsheba across from the roof of his palace. Noticing her wasn't wrong; anyone would have noticed her. She was provocatively good-looking. Glancing at her wasn't succumbing. Our temptation scale would say that perhaps one or two appreciative looks would have been all right. But David stared long and hard. As he stared, the temptation took on massive proportions and the invitation to sin became irresistible.

Learn to look away; it might save you the trouble of having to murder the husband later.

Defeating Temptation

In *The Hound of Everyman,* the play I mentioned in the opening of this chapter, Everyman finally defeats all the temptations by discovering a huge Bible, which he hides behind as a shield and wields as a weapon.

Nothing has changed. The Word of God is still our greatest weapon. We also have to dress ourselves in its armor.

As a navigating apprentice I joined my first ship, an oil tanker, in Naples where it had been dry-docked after a series of accidents. In one of these accidents, the ship's carpenter had gone down into the oil tanks to clean them without wearing the mandatory protection, an oxygen-breathing apparatus. The petroleum fumes, locked deep within the tanks of the hull, killed him. I always made sure that when it was my turn to clean the tanks I wore all the safety equipment.

In the same way, when you get ready to conquer temptation, wear the right equipment. "Put on the full armor of God so that you can take your stand against the devil's schemes" (Eph. 6:11).

Fight on, my friends.

Suggested reading:
White, John. "His Infernal Majesty," chapter 5 of *The Fight.* Downers Grove, Ill.: InterVarsity Press, 1976.
White, John. *Eros Defiled: The Christian and Sexual Sin.* Downers Grove, Ill.: InterVarsity Press, 1977.

7

Am I Normal?

At one time or another, haunted by a particular problem, most of us have stared at ourselves in the mirror and seriously wondered if we were normal. Something we've thought or done seems to have set us apart from our peers, and we begin to think we're weird.

A student friend, an actress, loved to rehearse her roles as she walked alone through a nearby park. One day, sitting by the edge of the lake and reciting Shakespeare out loud, she was suddenly confronted by an early morning rower, who anxiously asked, "Are you all right?" When you continually run into people who insist on asking "Are you all right?" you begin to wonder whether you are.

The worries of campus life can make us doubt our normality, and these doubts occur when our responses to situations are not the responses we are supposed to have. You may be fed up with school halfway through spring term and want to quit and become a commercial fisherman. Or you're bored stiff with all those carping, jellyfish Christians and don't care whether you ever go to a fellowship meeting again. Or you're so infatuated

"Oh Romeo, Romeo . . . "

---

with women's figures that you can't keep your eyes off them. Or you don't have any friends in the whole, wide world. Or you're so fascinated by chemistry that you could cheerfully stay in the lab for the rest of your life. Or you find that you're actually beginning to like modern dance and nihilistic novels and would sooner go to rehearsals than church.

Relax. I think you're pretty normal.

How Do I Compare?
Normality is a question of comparison. To ask, "Am I normal?" is to ask how I compare to everyone else. Do other Christian students feel the same way I do? Do they do the things I do? That's the normality problem. Am I different from everyone else or the same?

The answer to whether you're normal or not is often a yes and a no. Yes, because in the sweeping variety of human behavior there will always be some people who think and act the same way you do. Even within the narrower scope of the Christian church, you'll find people who are similar to you. Hundreds of students long to leave school in mid-February. And they don't want to go to church this Sunday either. I've said it before; I'll say it again. Relax. You're normal.

To define normality in these comparative terms is to take a statistical approach to the analysis of human behavior. Simply put, if enough other people think and do the same things you think and do, then you're all right; you're normal. Only when you can't find anyone else behaving the way you do, should you run off and borrow Fred's textbook on abnormal psychology.

The Normal Curve of Behavior

It might help us to understand this analytical approach if we learn about what statisticians call the "normal probability curve." We'll take IQ as an example (though IQ tests have their

The Normal Probability Curve and the Standard Deviation of Stanford-Binet IQ Scores

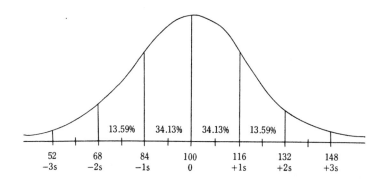

problems). Pretend that the question you are asking is, "Do I have a normal IQ?"

To answer your question, we'll have to find out what everyone else's IQ is. So we give the ten thousand people in your area standardized tests and record their scores.

There are no surprises in our data. Most people are average. They score about a hundred on the test. Some are just above and some below, while a few are exceptionally clever or dull.

This graph shows the distribution of IQ scores. The top numbers on the horizontal axis refer to the raw scores on the IQ tests. The percentages refer to the frequencies or proba- bilities of distribution. In other words, 50 per cent of the people score above 100 and 50 per cent score below 100. A score of 100 is therefore the mean score. However, 68.26 per cent of the population score between 84 and 116, whereas less than 1 per cent score either below 52 or above 148.

The lower numbers on the horizontal axis are an alternative way of expressing scores. Instead of using the raw scores from the IQ tests, statisticians can analyze data in terms of standard deviations, indicated by the +1, +2 and so on. To attain a score of 116, therefore, is to be one standard deviation above the mean (that is, the area from 100 to 116 on the graph is equivalent to one standard deviation).

You could say about any score, then, that to be between plus one and minus one standard deviation is to be very normal. To be above two standard deviations from the mean would be to score among the exceptional 4 per cent. Is your IQ normal? Check the graph and find out.

It's easy to do a normal probability curve with something measurable like IQ, height or the size of your feet. But how can this help you decide whether your fantasies about suicide, your dreams of your mother's death or your fears that you might be homosexual are normal?

Well, in a sense, we could still use the normal curve prin- ciple. Interviewing ten thousand students, we'd question them on their fantasies, dreams and sexual doubts. We might find that 74 per cent of students have thoughts in all three areas and that such thoughts occupy them for about five days per term.

Now, compare your behavior with the norm. If other students are having the same problems about as often as you, then you're perfectly normal.

So don't be too quick to think that you're weird. Although Christian students are naturally reticent about admitting their secret thoughts and actions, I believe that their range of behavior is wide enough to include all the things that sow doubt in your mind and cause you to worry.

Share Your Doubts

The following conversation took place at a student retreat.

"Hey, what's that book under your pillow?"

"Oh, er, nothing."

"Come on, let's have a look. What is it?"

"Oh, just a book I used to read when I was a kid."

"Used to read, eh? Well, what's it called?"

"It's, er, by A. A. Milne. You know, *Winnie-the-Pooh.*"

"What? You read about Pooh? Me too, I just love him."

"You do? What a relief. I thought you'd laugh at me. I thought I was the only living biology major who still read Pooh."

It is a great relief to meet another Christian student who has the same thoughts that cause you to doubt your normality. But unless you confide your fears to someone, you may never have the chance to be comforted by discovering that another person has exactly the same fears.

Finding someone else who reads *Winnie-the-Pooh* is very comforting at one level. But realizing that many Christian students are battling with masturbation, or actively dislike their parents, or have been rejected by two boyfriends or girl friends is a great relief. It's thinking that you are the only person in the whole world with such ideas in your head that is demoralizing. Therefore, I encourage you to share your disturbing thoughts with a counselor or friend or your local pastor.

Two Reference Groups

But I've said that the answer to the question "Am I normal?" is both yes and no. What do I mean by no—that you're a kook? Of course not. The key to normality is comparison, being like other people. It's not that you're like everybody, but that there are enough others doing the same thing to make your behavior normal.

The problem with being Christian is that you're wildly different. You don't tell lies and dirty jokes; you're not totally selfish and egocentric; you're not wild about money, ambition and status; you do the weirdest things like cleaning up after the all-night party and driving drunks home safely. If you compare yourself to the average student around you, you are marvelously different. You follow the ethic of Matthew 5—7 and belong to what John Stott has called the "Christian counter-culture."

So to be a normal Christian is to find strong similarities between you and the family of believers, but stark contrasts between you and the pagans around you. You have, therefore, two reference groups. By one, you must be measured normal; by the other, strange. It all depends who's measuring you. Let the world measure you by contrast and the kingdom by comparison.

Jesus sends you to the university to be salt and light. But if there are no differences between your so-called saltiness and the putrescence around you, if your light is so dim that it can hardly be detected in the moral gloom of the cafeteria, then you're abnormal from the Christian point of view.

So understand this clearly. Christians have thoughts and feelings that we share with all men and women. Following Jesus has not anesthetized our minds and emotions. We think and feel like all people. But as members of the new and invisible kingdom of Light, we have a revolutionary pattern of behavior and are consequently judged weird and strange by the standards of normality established in the culture around us.

Thus we have two reference groups. If the judgment of our pagan classmates is that we are absolutely normal in our behavior, this discounts any claim we might make with our tongues to be followers of Jesus. A teaching colleague once said to me, "Mike, you're a good man but you're weird. You've got to give up this Christianity nonsense." To him, I wasn't normal. Great . . . that's how it should be.

I've tried to show you that the thoughts and ideas that come into your mind and bring doubts about your normality are probably shared by all of us. But as followers of Jesus, we must guard ourselves carefully so that the unpleasant thoughts do not get translated into action. As with temptation, it is normal to think bizarre things, but if we nurse the thoughts and bring them to birth as actions, we are sinning. The Spirit's gift of self-control will help us to wrestle these ideas to the ground and eventually destroy them.

In Romans 12:2, Paul writes, "Do not conform any longer to the pattern of this world, but be transformed by the renewing of your mind." A renewed mind leads naturally to renewed behavior and a standard of normality that grows closer and closer to Jesus' standard of perfection.

Changing Clothes
Most of us have experienced the cleaning-up of mind and actions that accompanies this transformation process. My two daughters loved to play in mud and sand when they were five or six, soiling their jeans and T-shirts, scuffing their sneakers and muddying their faces and arms. But come time to go to a birthday party and the transformation was incredible. The faces were scrubbed and shiny, the hair brushed and combed, the dresses ironed and spotless. Now they couldn't accomplish this transformation by themselves. Their mother had to do it. But they had to want it for it to be thorough.

To be muddy and scruffy is normal for six-year-old children playing in the park. But as the context by which we judge normality changes from the park to the birthday party, so it's off with the patched shorts and on with the party dress. To be transformed by Jesus is to allow him to change our context for comparison and to put on us the new clothes of righteousness. What used to be normal must be discarded. The verb in the Romans text is passive: "be transformed." We must allow someone else to take charge of our being normal and dress us accordingly. But we must want it for it to be thorough.

I Still Think I'm Not Normal

I know that I've left some people out so far. When all the statistical evidence is in and you've found out how other students feel and think and you've been encouraged and so on, some doubts might still linger as to whether you're normal or not. What happens if you can not find anyone else who thinks your thoughts? What happens if you really do act differently? What then?

We should admit, without shame or embarrassment, without pity or mockery, that there are people whose behavior is not normal. There are people whose behavior is substantially different and in ways that are distressing to themselves, their families and friends. My encouragement to any of you who feel like this is to search for help among the members of the professional caring community.

Through a crisis line, in the pastor's office and the counseling department, there are dozens of competent, highly trained, honest and well-motivated people who can help you struggle with your problems of normality. These people are readily available. All you have to do is write, phone or call. And don't hesitate to do so. No sensible person would ever attach a stigma to you because you dropped in to see a counselor or made an appointment with a psychologist. Secular psychology does have validity for a Christian, and secular therapists can be helpful in interpreting the meaning of dreams, for example, or unraveling the repercussions of childhood trauma. Such professional help can lead to valuable insights into your own psyche and emotions.

Sometimes the appropriate thing to do is consult a Christian counselor. Such men and women understand readily the spiritual sources of self-doubt and can reconcile the biblical view of humanity with the wisdom gained by professional training. There is probably greater affinity, too, between a Christian student and a Christian counselor than between a Christian student and an unbelieving counselor who does not understand or has no sympathy with the Christian world view. You should feel free to explore the resources available and make your choice accordingly. Remember that many churches have pastoral care agencies; that Christian teachers in the psychology department can help you; and that your campus Christian leaders and Inter-Varsity staff will know with whom to put you in touch.

Normal but Not Ordinary

While we all long to be normal, none of us is interested in being ordinary. Our individuality cries out to be recognized. Good. Conformity and mediocrity are not qualities that Jesus calls for in his followers. He encourages us as we long, somehow, to be different—to be special. So our normality will always be spiced with idiosyncracies.

One of the counselors one year at Pioneer Pacific Camp— Inter-Varsity's summer camp for children on the Canadian west coast—was a young man who was hearing the voice of God calling him to be a missionary. In a talk with me, Scott shared some of his doubts about whether he was normal enough to be a missionary. Ever since childhood, he had felt different from the kids around him, different even from other young people in his church. They were establishment; he, somehow, was not. He didn't see himself fitting neatly into any of the service boxes that the church makes for people, least of all the box labeled "missionary." After all, how is there room in the establishment for a guy who rides a unicycle to school, reading the newspaper as he pedals?

In our talk, I told him how much I delighted in his individuality and how I saw it as a strength and a great gift from God. Who is more individualistic and nonconformist than a missionary who is willing to throw himself or herself into a totally foreign culture without any of the props of a normal life in a normal society? So the things that made Scott unique did not make him abnormal. Instead, they made him strong and authentic, a man whose uniqueness shone forth like a solo star in an empty, dark sky. In fact, a year after our talk, Scott was in Bolivia helping to run an evangelistic camp for Spanish-speaking children.

To me, the beautiful sights in life are the ones that are slightly different, the ones that are fresh and new. The sunset that is just a shade more orange than usual; the child whose face is more innocent than others; the man or woman whose goodness goes beyond the norm: these arrest me.

Jesus was different. He amazed the people who met him. Be a little different—for his sake.

Suggested reading:
Trobisch, Walter. *Love Yourself.* Downers Grove, Ill.: InterVarsity Press, 1976.
Peace, Richard. *Learning to Love Ourselves.* Downers Grove, Ill.: InterVarsity Press, 1968.

8

Summertime . . . the Livin' Is Easy

Porgy and Bess said it all. Summertime is when the living is easy. But while that might have been true for Gershwin and his all-star cast, it's probably less true for us. Summertime is not easy livin'. Although the prospect of three months' enforced idleness fills the heart with glee and although those three months that stretch enchantingly into the distance are probably the longest summer holiday you've had since kindergarten, the harsh reality is that summertime means work.

If you belong to one of those landed, rich families whose summers consist of alternating the tennis at Wimbledon with the rowing at Henley, ignore this next chapter and proceed straight to "Go." Do not collect $200; you don't need it. For the rest of you, for whom summer means making enough money to pay next year's tuition, read on.

Summer Plans Start in January

So you're three weeks into the January term and you're sensible enough to realize that you'd better think about the summer now. What are the best ways to plan ahead? I'd like to get at the question in two ways: the practical techniques for getting the summer organized into jobs and activities, and the attitude that ought to undergird all our summer planning.

The first thing to do is draw up a list of the things you'd like to accomplish during the summer vacation. Include all the things that are important to you. How much money do you need to make? Where do you want to spend the summer? At home reacquainting yourself with your parents or traveling through Mexico? How much rest and recreation do you need? Do you want to serve God in any particular ways? Will you have to take a summer-school course to pick up one you dropped or get a headstart on the calculus you need for second-year math?

Try to list all the things that are important or even interesting and then rank them in order of priority. Just as you rank your daily activities in terms of your goals and priorities (see chapter five), so your summer goals need to be organized as well. Put the most pressing needs at the top and the least at the bottom. There's nothing inherently evil in putting "make $4,000" at the top of the list. If God wants you in school and if that's what you need for school, then you must give it a high priority. Make your list carefully and prayerfully, because this order of priorities is going to dictate your planning.

And Continue in February

From February onward, start to work your way down that list, getting your items checked off one by one.

I have a hunch that for most of you the number one priority will be getting a job. I want to encourage you by saying that the opportunities are enormous. Don't get depressed by all those rumors about there being no jobs available. Those rumors are there year after year—and so are the jobs. I've never known a student who wasn't either fussy beyond words or paranoid about work who couldn't land a good job.

Stomp around the neighborhood and get some job information. Write letters to companies and make phone calls to the proper people. As well as contacting the personnel department, try to get hold of the boss who is in charge of the section you want to work in. In fact, the latter is probably more effective. The people to contact are the people who have authority to hire you. So get information. The more you know about mining in the Yukon or au-pairing in Geneva, the better it is. If you can call the right person, it's no waste of money to phone Geneva direct.

Another technique for getting information is to use the Christian network. There are brothers and sisters in every conceivable employment. Can you get hold of any local Christians in the Yukon? in Geneva? When I was emigrating to the city of Toronto, I knew no one in Canada. But I got in touch with a pastor in the city who put me up for a few nights, and I contacted Pioneer Camp in Ontario. They sent someone to meet me. The fact that he and I missed each other and I got lost is beside the point. The contacts I had made prior to arriving at the Toronto airport were invaluable.

Christian organizations such as Inter-Varsity Christian Fellowship and its international equivalent the International Fellowship of Evangelical Students are not employment agencies and are not to be used as such, but they do have all sorts of contacts. Someone may know about a vacancy at the University of Cairo that needs to be filled for the summer or about a hostel where you can volunteer in Spain. Or they may have summer activities planned that will interest you.[6] So use the Christian network intelligently.

All sorts of agencies publish booklets to help students find summer jobs. Check with employment agencies on your campus and in your community. Or check your local bookstores for listings of summer jobs here and abroad. Provincial and state governments create summer employment agencies. Service organizations also have information. The Canadian Bureau of International Education lists opportunities abroad and Inter-cristo, the Mennonite Central Committee and the Overseas

Counseling Service may be able to open up the world of summer missions.[7]

But remember your list of priorities. If number one is to make $4,000 to go to Osgoode Law School, then it's foolish to sign up as a volunteer at a youth camp on the French Riviera.

"Hi. I'm Bill, your counselor here at Camp Monaco. Should you need anything, I'll be right here."

There is lots of room for imagination and creativity in the business of landing a summer job. Several students I know here on the west coast have created their own business this summer. It is nothing very fancy: just odd-jobbing, remodeling, gardening and cleaning. They advertised in the newspapers. A girl took telephone inquiries and coordinated the crew of workers. Very quickly they had more work than they could handle.

Two other students who became an instant home redecorating firm were able to work sixteen hours a day, sometimes making as much as $1,000 per week. The fact that they chose to work long hours at the beginning meant that they could take time off to enter the North Thompson Raft Race (which they nearly won) and counsel for two weeks at Pioneer Pacific Camp. They stopped work by August and took a month off before school. One of them has now started a cross-country skiing school in British Columbia which he also uses as a means of evangelism. If you create your own company, you get the flexibility to do all sorts of other things besides work. But don't forget to start with those sixteen-hour days.

As you try to land that summer job, you may find you have to make trade-offs among your list of priorities. When a phone call to an executive in Montreal opens up the opportunity of a lifetime, you decide to forego priority number four (staying near home) to get number two (experience with computers). Be prepared to juggle your ambitions and adapt them as necessary, but don't throw away your number one.

So that's how to start. List the things you want to accomplish, rank them in order of priority and go after them one by one.

Adventurous Faith

What is the basic attitude you should have in your mind as you go about planning? I think it should be one of adventurous faith.

I want your attitude to be adventurous because I want to pry you away from the comfortable security that comes with working for Uncle Albert in the family grocery for the umpteenth time. Not that I'm against Uncle Albert or family groceries. But that's all so terribly safe. And I want you to be adventurous so that you can learn the ways of God. If you're not adventurous now, when you are young, when will you be? Let Uncle Albert give someone else an adventure this summer in his store while you wrap your belongings in a spotted handkerchief and hit the road to Fame and Fortune (population 135).

The three or four summer vacations that you'll get during your university career will give you some of the most marvelous opportunities for adventure that you'll ever have. Mine have led me from Edinburgh to Istanbul; from an armed forces assault course to an inner-city boys' club; from driving minibuses to digging ditches; from garbage duty to security patrol. For those three months, you have the choice of what you're going to do, and the world is open to you. Best of all, the Lord who owns you also owns the world—the entire thing is his. From the research job in the library to the deck of a gillnetter out of Prince Rupert, this world belongs to him. And he has a summer place for you.

Do you need to make tuition money? There are adventurous ways to do that. You need to live at home with your folks? There are adventurous ways to do that. With their capital and your inventive genius, go into a dressmaking business and do a fashion show at the local community center. You want to take the grand tour of Europe? There are many adventurously unselfish ways to do that too.

I am not thinking of adventure in the glamorous *Nurse Roger's Holidays in Rome* style of a Harlequin Romance or the heroic style of disaster movies like *Towering Inferno*. Of course, there is adventure in romance and disaster, and I hope you get a taste of both of them. I am still hopelessly lost in romance (what a marriage I made), and I found high adventure when I drove into Skopje in Yugoslavia hours after a terrible earthquake.

I think of adventure as a quality of the radical, Christian life. Adventures befall those who are seriously following Jesus. A friend of mine found himself trailing a student from Japan through the city streets at midnight, trying to prevent him from falling into the clutches of a drug peddler. Another found himself invading a sleazy bar in an attempt to rescue his drunken secretary from a night that promised disaster. When he was cautioned by a more conservative friend about what others might say, his reply was, "They might say I'm like Jesus."

Jesus calls us to that same crazy, reckless selflessness and generosity that got the twelve disciples into so much trouble.

I want you to get into trouble during your summer vacation—trouble for Jesus' sake. Throw yourself with abandon into this wildest of all adventures, the Christian adventure. Forget your comfort and your safety and let God stretch you.

This is where faith comes in. I'm not countenancing foolish recklessness; I'm arguing for adventurous faith. "Trust in the Lord with all your heart and lean not on your own understanding; in all your ways acknowledge him, and he will make your paths straight" (Prov. 3:5-6). Believing in God's concern for your summer job and his ability to guide you to one is enormously helpful in taking the panic and foolishness out of your adventure.

You have to believe that God's guidance for you is good; not necessarily gentle or safe or comfortable. In this excerpt from *The Lion, the Witch and the Wardrobe* by C. S. Lewis, Lucy and Susan (children who inexplicably find themselves in the animal land of Narnia) are questioning Mr. and Mrs. Beaver about the mysterious being called Aslan. In this fantasy, Aslan represents Christ.

"Is he a man?" asked Lucy.

"Aslan a man!" said Mr. Beaver sternly. "Certainly not. I tell you he is the King of the world and the son of the Emperor-Beyond-the-Sea. Don't you know who is the King of Beasts? Aslan is a lion—*the* Lion, the great Lion."

"Ooh!" said Susan, "I'd thought he was a man. Is he—quite safe? I shall feel rather nervous about meeting a lion."

"That you will, dearie, and no mistake," said Mrs. Beaver, "if there's anyone who can appear before Aslan without their knees knocking, they're either braver than most or else just silly."

"Then he isn't safe?" said Lucy.

"Safe?" said Mr. Beaver. "Don't you hear what Mrs. Beaver tells you? Who said anything about safe? 'Course he isn't safe. But he's good. He's the King, I tell you."[8]

So it is not safety that is to be your prime concern, but goodness.

It has been said that you can pray your way out of trouble. That may be so. But I want you to learn how to pray your way into trouble—how to pray your way into joining the adventure of faith. Prayer can open up all sorts of ways for you to get involved in the work of God's kingdom. A friend of mine, having as his top priority the need to be free in July so that he might counsel at Pioneer Ranch Camp in Alberta, refused several jobs that would not permit him to take July off. He was beginning to despair, but he continued to pray. The next employer, after offering good wages and interesting work, apologetically admitted that there was a snag, "We'll have to lay you off in July." Prayer does that sort of thing, you know.

Witness and Service

Two features will identify those students who are on the road of adventurous faith. These are witness and service. If you cannot get a summer filled with those two activities, you've missed the call. So paint your houses for $1,000 per week, but throw in free service to the Vietnamese refugee family that just settled in your city. Do your odd-job gardening but let your clients know who it is you really work for. Make your thousands in the mines of north Saskatchewan to go to law school in Toronto, but start a small group Bible study in the bunkhouse, even if that small "group" begins with just two of you. Go to Europe but call in at Schloss Mittersill for a conference and visit a L'Arche community to wash dishes for three weeks. Get a vision for the whole starving, fractured world. Feed it and patch it up. That's your task. Carry your bandages and use them all over the globe, in the name of Jesus who heals and reconciles all things.

I'd like you to make that your summer job. Rewrite your list of priorities and put at the top, "Patching up the world for Jesus' sake." You will have to use your faith to do this. You will have to believe that when you rewrite your priorities to conform to the standards of the kingdom, God does something in return.

Well, what does God do? Make a note of your name and address and file it? Put you on hold? Tell you not to call him, he'll call you? None of these. As you bring to the top of your list the genuine desire to get involved in adventurous faith, God smiles to himself and brings out his gifts. Because as you commit yourself to him, he commits himself to you and equips you for the job. And he will not be your debtor; he will unload on you some of the marvels and glories and pains of his kingdom. Watch out—it might hurt. But you will love it, and you will grow.

Now how can God respond to you if you still insist on putting "work at Uncle Albert's grocery" at the top of your list? It's hard for God to pull out anything imaginative in that situation. There's no risk, and when there's no risk there's little room for God to stretch and teach you. That's one reason why Jesus sent the disciples out on the road without their suitcases instead of letting them set up a study institute at the University of Jerusalem.

Christian Gambling?

Take a risk this summer. That's my plea in a sentence. Be like the adventurous servant in the parable of the talents (Mt. 25:14-30). What do you want to do at the end of August when you face God on your way to your next year in school? Reluctantly unscrew your fist and show him the single talent, earthy from having been buried, creased from having been clenched secretly and tightly in your hand? Or bring fistfuls of talents, risked, speculated, doubled and tripled through a summer of adventurous faith?

Gambling your life in Christ's service is not so reckless as it seems. It would be if God were incompetent or foolish or simply not quite able to cope with things anymore. But in recklessly throwing yourself into his hands you are putting yourself in the charge of the sovereign Lord of the universe, the One who creates and sustains, the One who speaks and it is so. He is the One who said he would never leave nor forsake you. "And surely

I will be with you always, to the very end of the age" (Mt. 28:20). He is the one from whom nothing in heaven or hell or all creation can separate us (Rom. 8:38-39).

Suggested reading:

Smith, Blaine. *Knowing God's Will: Biblical Principles of Guidance.* Downers Grove, Ill.: InterVarsity Press, 1979.

Student Missionary Union. *Summer Mission Opportunities.* Published yearly by Biola College, 13800 Biola Ave., La Mirada, Calif. 90639.

White, John. "Deliverance from Drudgery," chapter 10 of *The Fight.* Downers Grove, Ill.: InterVarsity Press, 1976.

9

Nothing Succeeds like Success

Well, did you make it? Did you pass your year, I mean? You got two A's and three B's? Congratulations. You did make it.

But you failed at some things, didn't you? You would be superhuman and extraordinary if you didn't. We all fail at some things, even those of us who win Rhodes Scholarships or become the number one college draftee for the Montreal Alouettes.

To start with the most obvious area, some of you flunked a course or two. Perhaps you tried your best all year, or perhaps you gave up after that horrendous midterm in February. Whatever, the result is the same—an F. And some of you are disappointed at your failures in athletics. You really wanted to be the top goalie on the varsity hockey team, and you lost your place to that mouthy whizzkid from Quebec.

There have probably been relationships that have soured on you. You tried so hard to trust and respect that insecure teaching assistant, but his incompetence drove you away, and you made him mad. Or you've fallen in and out of love so fast that the stars in your eyes hardly had time to twinkle. Or you have been rejected by someone you really admired; you have broken off any last hopes for getting on with your parents; or you have driven your roommate out into the snow muttering darkly about the baser sides of your personality.

"*#&!*?!"

For some of you, the failures have been what you would call more directly spiritual. You have stopped going to the Bible study meetings, and you duck furtively around the corner when any Christian who knows you comes into view. You have taken out the *D* from the DQT that you initiated with such determination on January 1. In fact, your Quiet Time has become so quiet now that no one can hear it, not even God.

And what happened to that great schedule that you drew up for yourself at the beginning of term, clearly showing how you were going to plan your days so you would achieve more than any other student in the history of the world? All that has happened since is that you can't even find time to read the schedule, let alone put it into practice. And in a sense, you don't want to read it because there are godly ambitions there which would dismay you if you read them again now. You probably share the same fate as Samuel Johnson, the famous creator of the first acknowledged English dictionary. It was said about him, when he was at Oxford University: "He prepared a detailed programme of work, calculating how much he would have to get through each day to read what he ought to read; yet he could never settle down to it."[9] He only lasted one year at Oxford.

And like all people, you have probably failed at one time or another to stand against the temptations of the Enemy. So now, even to be reminded of that floods you with guilt and shame. You wonder if you can ever be forgiven for it or whether you have really confessed it enough, or whether you should seek some reconciliation or make reparation. And you wonder if God will ever love you again.

What Did Failure Teach You This Year?
The good thing about failure is that it teaches you something. It teaches you what you can't do. The sure-fire way to learn that you cannot jump across a certain chasm is to try it . . . and fail. As you tumble headlong into the abyss you can mumble to yourself, "Well, at least I learned something."

You have learned this year, then, that there are some skills you just do not have. After eight months of mathematics, you know that you simply do not have the expertise to pass Calculus 130. Or in more general terms, you do not have the basic aptitude for math that is likely to give you success if you follow an honors math degree.

So if there is any value in failing a course or not being chosen for a varsity team or not having your Super 8 creative movie accepted for an Arts Award, that value lies in coming to an honest and guiltless awareness of your lack of skill in that area. There is no need to be alarmed or ashamed at that. Everyone is bad at something; no one is good at everything. Winston Churchill failed his Latin courses at school. Albert Einstein failed math.

If you do not believe that everyone fails at something, check around. Ask your friends what sort of things they have failed since kindergarten. (Some might even have failed kindergarten!) I failed a music exam, an interview to become a probation officer and a whole lot more.

I would suggest, with some caution, that a lot of the things you failed are unimportant and can simply be left behind you. A dropped course, a lost game, a loused-up schedule—all these are not eternally significant. You can leave them behind.

Some things, however, are important; too important to leave behind. That is why there are such things as make-ups. If you're just about graduating from medicine and you only got 49% on your final histology exam, then you have to go back and do it again, with gratitude for the second chance.

By and large, the context of your specific failure will determine whether you have to go back and repeat the test. If your failure is off in left field somewhere, a delectable elective by which you were wildly tempted (say, Medieval Economics with a lab in Serfdom), such a context suggests that it is unimportant. If the failed test lies at the core of your future ambitions, then you might have to sign up for summer school straight-away. (Who wants to be operated on by a surgeon who got 51% on the final?)

I am not suggesting, then, that you can simply fly away from all failure. I think that you can from most, but there are certainly some areas and issues that need to be tried again and again.

What about Spiritual Failure?
Failure in the area of Christian obedience is an issue that cannot be lightly forgotten or deemed unimportant. How do you deal, therefore, with the temptations that have defeated you and the godly ambitions you have discarded like crumpled McDonald's wrappers?

The first thing to do is to make sure that the weakness, the error—let's use the right word—the sin, is clearly looked at and confessed. To kneel down and read aloud Psalm 51 or recite the general confession from the Book of Common Prayer are excellent ways of articulating your confession. Both these prayers probably need to be complemented by a very specific confession of those particular sins that are in your memory as you read the words.

To absolve yourself by confession is to involve yourself in forgiveness. Confession and forgiveness are linked like sugar and sweetness. To pour sugar into a drink is to create sweetness just as your confession before God lets loose his flood of forgiveness. They are linked as a match and its flame are linked. To strike the match of confession is to receive the flame of forgiveness. Isn't this exactly what 1 John 1:9 is all about?

But you may doubt that God will forgive you. You might torture your mind as to the sincerity and extent of your confession. Am I really sorry, you worry. Am I sorry enough? Can God really forgive me for doing that? *Me* for doing *that?*

Let me tell you that the death of Christ on the cross was designed, in part, for that very purpose. For the very purpose of attaining forgiveness for you for exactly the things that you think are unforgiveable. As God saw with peerless insight into the future, as he foresaw the extent of the sin even of those men and women who would begin to believe and begin to follow, he saw that the enormity of the problem necessitated an enormous answer. That is what the death of Christ is: it is the Enormous Solution to the problem of evil. It is the cosmic expunction of guilt. Do you think that your individual error and weakness are too large for that?

Stand firm on the climax of Peter's apologetic in Acts 5:30-31: "The God of our fathers raised Jesus from the dead—whom you had killed by hanging him on a tree. God exalted him to his own right hand as Prince and Savior that he might give repentance and forgiveness of sins to Israel."

Move on, my friends. You're clean.

You Did Well at Some Things
Your year wasn't a total failure, was it? You did succeed at some
things. In fact, you were excellent in that chemistry course and
you scored the winning point in the intramural volleyball
final. You have had a strong and growing Quiet Time this year,
and you know God better now than ever before. You witnessed
to a friend, and you fell in love . . . and stayed fallen!

I am sure that for most of you, this year in college has brought
you a large amount of success. Some of it has not surprised
you—you have always been good at chemistry. But some of the
good things that have happened have taken you aback. You
never knew that you'd be so good at home economics, that you
would enjoy interior design so very much.

Why don't you draw up an inventory of your talents? Think
through the year, bring back to mind all the successes you have
had (even if it will only take ten seconds) and write them down.
You can group them in categories such as: academic, athletic, lei-
sure, church and so on. Then, in front of your very eyes, you will
have a talent profile of yourself. You'll know what you're good at.

This is useful for a couple reasons. It might help you to know
yourself better, and it might be useful in planning further
studies and your vocational future. For those of you who have
fallen in love "and stayed fallen," it might be enjoyable and
profitable for you to write out the talent sheet profile as a pair,
in conjunction with the person you love.

The next stage after making the profile is to see if you can
rank your abilities in order of importance. To have won the
men's residence blackjack, table tennis and skateboard tourney
is good fun, but to have carried off the president's prize in
English literature might be more important when it comes to
knowing yourself and making career decisions.

Inevitably, too, you are going to have to make tradeoffs.
You will possibly end up having to drop Spanish guitar, which
you really love and brings an easy success, to concentrate on
your oboe, because your ambition is to play oboe with the

Chicago Symphony. And to have some sort of evaluative hierarchy as to which are your more important gifts will help you make those tradeoffs.

Another advantage of listing the things that you succeeded at, especially in terms of relating to and serving people, is to give you an idea of where your spiritual gifts might lie and how you can serve the church. I was delighted to find this principle demonstrated in the church I joined after moving to Vancouver. Each newcomer is encouraged to fill out a "talent sheet" and return it to the rector. These talents are, of course, related to the ones in Jesus' parable of the talents and to the lists of spiritual gifts. The rector does not want to know if you are a song-and-dance man who can play Gershwin.

Finally, as you create your talent profile, try to keep yourself, your talents and successes, in perspective. Paul urges us, "Do not be proud. . . . Do not be conceited" (Rom. 12:16). He continues by saying, "Do nothing out of selfish ambition or vain conceit, but in humility consider others better than yourselves" (Phil. 2:3).

My life has been much enriched through the friendship of four professional musicians who play in the Victoria Symphony Orchestra, all of whom are among the foremost performers in the country. You have to be excellent to get any sort of job in an orchestra for this is a highly competitive profession.

Their musical skill and expertise are impressive. But what impresses me more than anything else is their immense modesty, graciousness and generosity. They state clearly that their talents are gifts from God and that it is in reflection of his creativity that they have developed their musicianship. They claim that they are the stewards of their skills, not the owners of them. They give freely of themselves, sharing their profound musical expression with whomever will listen.

I love modesty. As you clearly and rightly recognize that you are gifted in certain areas, remember that the word is *gifted*. Success has been granted to you by Someone else. In other words, your talents are from God, and if anyone is to boast of anything, it is of the generous favor of God who bestows gifts on all his creatures and who offers us his Son for our redemption. "May I never boast," Paul's voice rings out, "except in the cross of our Lord Jesus Christ, through which the world has been crucified to me, and I to the world" (Gal. 6:14).

What Does It Mean to Succeed?

Success is usually measurable. A student sets as her goal the achievement of a B+ in history. If she gets that mark, she is successful; if she doesn't get it, she has failed. So you can score much success like you score soccer results.

If I were to ask you whether your year was successful as a Christian, how would you reply? What does it mean to be a successful Christian? Is it measurable at all?

I think we have to start with the goal. What is the goal of a Christian student throughout the year at college?

I can find no better answer than the one I learned from a study of Philippians 3. The goals that are suitable for a Christian student are the ones that are suitable to all of us as we strain to make a success out of our discipleship.

First of all, Paul distinguishes two sets of values: those from this political and material world, values of status, education, ambition; and those from another world, the value of finding and knowing Christ. Then he says clearly that he has rejected the former values and willingly substituted for them the values and goals of the other world, the kingdom of God. "Whatever was to my profit [arising out of my ordinary life]," he says, "I now consider loss. . . . I consider everything a loss compared to the surpassing greatness of knowing Christ Jesus my Lord" (vv. 7-8).

So that is the first step in forming the goal of Christian discipleship. We have to consciously reject status seeking in society as the overriding, consuming ambition of life and grasp with all firmness the fact that our ambition as believers, our goal, is to know Christ. Therefore, the process of measuring Christian success consists of measuring to what extent we have grown in our knowledge of Christ.

"I want to know Christ," cries Paul passionately, "and the power of his resurrection and the fellowship of sharing in his sufferings" (v. 10). The agony and the ecstasy. Most of us would happily embrace this goal if we could settle for the power and avoid the suffering. Is it possible to do that? In fact, some people would say that the measure of success is the extent to which we have managed to avoid the suffering. Is that true?

No. The measure of success is the extent to which we know both the resurrection and the suffering of Jesus Christ. The paradoxical duality of this image is with us everywhere: the joys and pains of falling in love, the meetings and partings of friendship, the strength and vulnerability of commitment. We cannot choose only the nice things and ignore the nasty. To be involved in God's rescue strategy for the universe is to be metaphorically digging in the earthquake rubble with our bare hands or working waist-deep in the flood waters.

To know this power and suffering is not to have taken part in a particular event, to have achieved a particular end or to have attained a particular level or stage. Knowledge of Christ is the destination at the end of a highway. No one has yet arrived, not even Paul, for he openly admits he has not yet attained the end (Phil. 3:13).

So your Christian success on campus this year is not to be assessed by anything you have actually done or completed or achieved. Your success is not vested finally and absolutely in the fact of your daily fifty-minute Quiet Time, your leadership of a great Bible study, your reading of sixteen devotional classics, your leading three friends to Christ or your meteoric rise toward holiness. Your success as a Christian on campus is measured by the direction you are moving with regard to knowing the power and suffering of Christ.

We are all running a race of one kind or another, all moving

fundamentally toward Christ or away from him. If you are in
the race that is running toward the crucified, living and glorified
Lord of the universe, then you are successful. Some of you might
squirm a little at this, wanting to be more explicitly fussy,
wanting to measure the amount of track you have covered since
September, wanting to compute your speed over the distance.
Speed is not the point; direction is everything. Forget what lies
behind, face the right direction and press on. "One thing I do:
Forgetting what is behind and straining toward what is ahead, I
press on toward the goal to win the prize for which God has called
me heavenward in Christ Jesus" (Phil. 3:13-14).

The Christian Race

The image that the Christian life is like a race is one that is
developed by Paul in two places in the New Testament. In the
first three verses of Hebrews 12, he emphasizes the perseverance
that is necessary as we strain toward the finish line, which is
Christ. In 1 Corinthians 9:24-27, he comments on the single-
minded devotion to a task that characterizes both the athlete
and the disciple. Let me develop that image as a conclusion
to this chapter and to the book.

I have learned a lot about running from my own experiences
with the sport. I have learned that training is both essential
and difficult. It is especially difficult in the winter, when it is
cold, and you run past all those houses with their warm lights
on, wondering just what you're missing. You smell the cedar
smoke from the fireplaces; you see a child setting the dinner
table; you watch with envy as people arrive home from work
and are received with hugs and kisses into the bright rectangle
of light. You clench your fists inside your mitts, force your
head away from the house and continue counting your steps
into the darkness.

Winter darkness is depressing; running in the dark can be
almost suicidal. I've had to jump aside on more than one oc-
casion from the blinding glare of an oncoming car, finding

myself momentarily stumbling in a ditch and furious with the motorist.

Christians must train and run in the light. We are to avoid secret habits and dark thoughts and the deeds of shame that dare only be done at night. Our race is in the open honesty of the stadium, where spectators can watch and examine and be persuaded of our talents. To run in the light is the metaphor that John uses in his letter to describe our obedience to the Father. Be encouraged by his promise that "the darkness is passing and the true light is already shining" (1 Jn. 2:8).

Then there are the dogs—the jogger's curse. I don't think I have ever been so angry in my life as I was when a vicious, little nondescript dog sunk his teeth into my calf as I was jogging along the seawalk in Victoria. The nasty dogs are easy to recognize: like the obvious temptations of life, they bark in furious anger, determined to trip or bite us and cause our downfall. I have a sure-fire technique for dealing with such animals—I turn around and jog in the opposite direction. I'm not going to give any of them the satisfaction of biting me again.

Some dogs, though, are merely friendly. They just want to run with you for a while. But they can be as dangerous as the ones who bark ferociously, roll their eyes in anger and chase you out of the neighborhood. I lived on a farm one year, and jogging back home meant running up a quarter-mile driveway through the fields to the house. The four farm dogs would greet me joyously at the bottom of the driveway, leaping around, jumping unrestrainedly and barking happily. All in fun, of course, and doggy devotion.

The problem was that they would invariably get underneath my feet and trip me. I had a couple of dangerous falls that way. So I learned that friendly dogs are as dangerous as unfriendly ones. And the dogs you meet on your Christian training runs will also come in various guises. Beware of all temptations, impediments and obstacles—even those disguised as friends. They do nothing but trip and bite.

There is encouragement for the lonely jogger, panting his or her way through the park, dodging the dogs. It came for me in many ways: the cheerful wave from a passing runner; the pleasure of the exercise itself; some great scenery as I ran along the cliffs beside the sea; being welcomed home to a hot shower and supper; having my daughter meet me at the bottom of the driveway and run the final distance with me. So also in your Christian race, there is warm companionship (just think how many other runners are in the same race) and great encouragement.

The Race Itself

Competitors need to make sure that they are in the right race and that they do not miss the start. In the 1972 Olympics in Mexico, the two favored American sprinters missed the start of the 100-meter final because their coach got his timetable mixed up. For them, there was no second chance. For a high-school student I know, who arrived late at the starting line of a cross-country race (delayed by a nervous dash to the washroom), there was the sight of the other competitors' backs receding around the first turn three hundred meters away. For him, there was hope still, but it is difficult to start when you know that you are three hundred meters behind already.

Actually, the start is not of supreme value in our competition. The 100-meter dash, in which the start is absolutely crucial, is not the biblical image of the Christian race. Running to know Christ is more along the lines of a middle-distance race or even a marathon. We have all started with greater or lesser ease and speed—with believing parents and godly upbringings or hostile childhoods and abused adolescences. It matters not greatly the manner of our start; the race goes to those who endure, not to those who have put in a fabulous start.

Endurance is possibly the key to the whole thing. For many of us, the Christian race seems most like the third lap of a four-lap race. This lap is the one called the "killer lap." You're too far into the race to quit now; you've been semisprinting for two laps. Your legs feel like lead and your lungs like iron. You're hurting, and if it wasn't almost over you'd give up on the spot. Yet you aren't close enough to the end to pick up the psychological lift of the finishing tape and the roar of the crowd. All you do is endure, forcing your legs to keep pounding down the track, grimly determined. To keep running is to succeed.

If you feel as if you are only, still, perhaps always, in the third lap, the only way to encourage you is to promise you that there will, eventually, be a final lap and a finishing line. But the only route to the rewards of the fourth lap is through the agony of the third.

What of the finishing line? Well of course, none of us meets it till we die, till we leave the race on this planet to take part in that final sprint of joy. If it is as yet unknown, it will be familiar. There will be friends at the tape; old training partners and a coach or two we knew. There will be cheering and excitement beyond description as the stands erupt in happiness. And there will be rest as we lie panting on the grass in the center oval. There will be the sort of things and the sort of people we thought would be there; and the race will be over. And—miracle of miracles—we all will have won!

Are You Still Running?

It probably seems a long time ago that you started your year at college. It might be even longer ago when you started your life as a believer and disciple and signed on for the Christian race. The question is, were you successful? Are you still running in the race toward knowledge of Jesus Christ?

One of the standard acts of nostalgia for immigrants, such as I, is to return to "the old country" to check up on old friends. For a Christian, this can sometimes be a sad experience. Time after time you realize that good old Al, who used to run the youth group at church, has abandoned his faith and dropped out of the race; Phyllis, who was a dynamic witness to your high school, is now sitting in the stands watching the runners.

To endure is to be successful. Jesus said so. "He who stands firm to the end will be saved" (Mt. 10:22). Paul, when he had finished using his metaphor of the race in Philippians 3, said, "Therefore, my brothers, you whom I love and long for, my joy and crown, that is how you should stand firm in the Lord" (4:1).

One day, at the craziest awards banquet you could ever conceive, you will receive your prize.

Suggested reading:
Campolo, Anthony, Jr. *The Success Fantasy.* Wheaton, Ill.: Victor Books, 1980.

Notes

[1] (London: Pan Books Ltd., 1978), p. 110.

[2] It is sad to say that Christian students must be careful these days about what groups they join on campus. Many cult groups have recruiting organizations which work to win students' trust and lure them into counterfeit spirituality. The Local Church and The Way International are both groups whose beliefs are very close to, but divergent from, orthodox Christianity. They often hold Bible studies and seminars on campuses. Local Church groups frequently carry names such as "Christians at _____ University."

The Unification Church of Sun Myung Moon also recruits on campuses. Students will be attracted to discussion groups on interesting topics, including religion and the meaning of life. They may be unaware that these discussions are being led by Moonies. Once students show interest, they might be invited to go on cheap vacations or attend weekend seminars where more intensive instruction may be given.

Students wishing to avoid being misled or recruited into such groups should do a little research. If a group does not carry a familiar title such as Inter-Varsity, Navigators, Campus Crusade, or indicate denominational ties such as Baptist Student Union (Southern Baptist), Canterbury Club (Episcopal) or Newman Club (Roman Catholic), you should ask to see a statement of faith and get to know the local leader.

If the members cannot give you a clear, definite statement of what they believe, you should be wary.

Literature on some of these organizations is available at your local bookstore or by writing InterVarsity Press (5206 Main St., Downers Grove, IL 60515, USA or 1875 Leslie St., Unit 10, Don Mills, Ontario M3B 2M5, Canada) or the Spiritual Counterfeits Project (Box 2418, Berkeley, CA 94702).

[3]You can subscribe to the monthly Scripture Union bulletins by writing them at: 1716 Spruce St., Philadelphia, PA 19103 *or* 300 Steel Case Rd. West #19, Markham, Ontario L3R 2W2, Canada.

[4]For information on *This Morning with God* and other Bible study aids, ask for a catalog from InterVarsity Press.

[5]InterVarsity Press has many helpful books to aid students in understanding and recognizing various world views. *Developing a Christian Mind* and *The Universe Next Door* are two such titles.

[6]In North America, Inter-Varsity itself runs many summer activities that focus on student leadership. Canadian IVCF organizes Pioneer Camps in Ontario, Manitoba, Alberta and British Columbia which offer recreational evangelistic challenges for children. These are staffed largely by college students. Some of the Canadian divisions run a summer training experience called Campus-in-the-City, a live-in community experience or direct summer missions program without that live-in element. For information, write IVCF, 745 Mt. Pleasant Rd., Toronto, Ontario M4S 2N5, Canada.

American IVCF also offers a variety of summer training camps throughout the nation for college students. These include New Testament seminars, camps for small group leaders, discipleship training schools and projects focusing on reaching particular areas for Christ, such as inner-city Boston, Aspen, Salt Lake City and Mackinac Island. For information, see your local staff member or write IVCF, 233 Langdon St., Madison, WI 53703.

[7]Here are some addresses for you:

Overseas Counseling Service, 1594 North Allen #23, Pasadena, CA 91104.

Mennonite Central Committee—USA, 21 South 12th St., Akron, PA 17501.

Mennonite Central Committee—Canada, 201-1483 Pembina Highway, Winnipeg, Manitoba R3T 2C8.

Intercristo, P.O. Box 9323, Seattle, WA 98109.

Canadian Bureau of International Education, 151 Slater St., Ottawa, Ontario K1P 5H3.

[8]New York: Collier Books, 1950, pp. 75-76.

[9]Christopher Hibbert, *The Personal History of Sam: Johnson* (London: Longman, 1971), p. 18.